A Soundtrack for Life

A Soundtrack for Life

Classical Music to Take You Through the Day

Kyle Books

An Hachette UK Company
www.hachette.co.uk

First published in Great Britain in 2021 by
Kyle Books, an imprint of Octopus Publishing Group Limited
Carmelite House
50 Victoria Embankment
London EC4Y 0DZ
www.kylebooks.co.uk
www.octopusbooksusa.com

ISBN: 9780857839671

Distributed in the US by Hachette Book Group,
1290 Avenue of the Americas, 4th and 5th Floors, New York, NY 10104

Distributed in Canada by Canadian Manda Group,
664 Annette St., Toronto, Ontario, Canada M6S 2C8

Publishing Director: Judith Hannam
Publisher: Joanna Copestick
Editor: Jenny Dye
Jacket design: Steve Leard
Design and typesetting: Peter Ward

A Cataloguing in Publication record for this title is available from the British Library

Printed and bound in the UK

10 9 8 7 6 5 4 3 2 1

The FSC® label means that materals used for the product
have been responsibly sourced.

CONTENTS

FOREWORD
by Simon Mayo

Classical Music for Modern Life – that's how we like to refer to Scala Radio. But what does it actually mean, away from the management meetings with executive types and media influencers?

Well, the book you have in your hands will give you a strong flavour of our intentions to bring classical music well and truly into the here and now. Scala Radio believes that classical music is all around us, and is for everyone. We love classical music in all its shapes, sizes and guises, and we love to share our passion for the music over the airwaves every single day, whether it's a masterpiece from the Baroque era or a pop hit reworked by a moody, finely chiselled French pianist.

However, we're acutely aware that for some people, classical music can feel like an impenetrable fortress, guarded by formidable, sniffy folk who don't welcome the likes of us. Where, exactly, is the best place to begin? Well, hello! That's where *A Soundtrack for Life* comes in.

This is a collection of classical and classically inspired pieces grouped around occasions or themes. From life-changing moments such as weddings and births to everyday activities like walking the dog, washing the dishes and going to sleep. You'll find short descriptions about each piece of music, with nuggets of information about when it was written, why the composer wrote it, how it sounds, and how it has been received by audiences.

Arranged in this way, *A Soundtrack for Life* highlights the different roles a piece of music can play in our lives: music as entertainment, music with a message, music for solace, music for celebration, music for music's sake. It all serves a purpose.

This is very much a Scala Radio compilation, spanning the centuries. Bach, Mozart, Rachmaninov and Florence Price nestle comfortably alongside Lady Gaga, King Crimson, The Style Council and Aphex Twin. That's quite a playlist! Symphonies, concertos and choral works rub shoulders with film, TV and video game soundtracks. Other musical elements like folk, jazz, world and electronica can be found within some of the selected pieces, proving yet again that classical music has influenced – and been influenced by – other genres. It's not an island, but, as my old geography teacher would have said, a continually evolving ecosystem. (He would also have been amazed to know I was paying attention.)

As for me, I've discovered so much about my own musical tastes since presenting shows on Scala Radio. When I joined the station for the launch in March 2019, my love for Mozart was well and truly thriving, but it was such a joy to find fresh new takes on his works, most notably horn player Sarah Willis' impressively lively genre-merging album *Mozart y Mambo* – one of my favourite releases of 2020. Thanks to Scala, I've discovered choral works by Jaakko Mantyjarvi, and I've learned that I'm a huge fan of big shouty choirs performing works by Grieg and Handel. Once you've heard the big shouty versions, everything else seems rather feeble I find.

I've always been a fan of film scores and it's been a pleasure to play the soundtracks from the likes of 1917 by Thomas Newman, *Joker* by Hildur Guðnadóttir and everything by Max Richter on Scala Radio. My esteemed colleague (his choice of words) Mark Kermode's passion for movie music is unparalleled and if you regularly join him for his fabulous Scala Radio show, you'll appreciate just how far he likes to stretch the concept of 'classical' and indeed 'music' with his selections! Whether your 'way in' to classical music was a record of Beethoven's Symphony No. 6 – as it was for me – or a showtune from a musical, a theme from a video game, a track used in an advert, The Wombles, Barry Manilow's love of Chopin or Billy Joel's use of Beethoven, there's room for everyone. Even 'media influencers'.

I hope *A Soundtrack for Life* will allow you to discover more about the music you know and love – and to discover new favourites too. Try this. Open it at random. Stab a finger at a page. Find that piece of music. Press play.

And we're off again . . .

Simn May

INTRODUCTION

Scala Radio is a classical music and entertainment radio station, home to Angellica Bell, Mark Kermode, Penny Smith, Alexis Ffrench, Simon Mayo and more. We love to showcase classical music from the Baroque era to the present day, playing familiar masters such as Mozart, Beethoven and Bach alongside contemporary works including film, TV and video game scores, showtunes from musicals and instrumental reworkings of pop and rock songs by the likes of Beyoncé, Led Zeppelin and Dua Lipa.

As well as offering a broad range of classical sounds and styles – something for everyone, classical music aficionados and newcomers alike – we like to reflect your lives and lifestyles. If you're looking for a gentle start to your day, try 'In The Park', every morning between 5–7am, with calming music and natural soundscapes like birdsong. There are also regular 'Mindfulness Music' sections within the shows, offering you a bit of time out and headspace thanks to a selection of peaceful classical compositions. Likewise, if you need something rousing to kickstart the weekend, make a date with Friday Night Scala, a show packed full of lively pieces we like to refer to as 'classical bangers'! We love live music and supporting both established and up-and-coming musical talent, so we broadcast exclusive live Scala Sessions every week and showcase brand new releases every Friday in the imaginatively titled 'New Release Friday'!

Scala Radio aims to be a breath of fresh air in the world of classical music radio. We don't feel the need to treat the music with kid gloves, speaking in hushed, reverent tones, nor do we think the listener wants to hear the same well-known pieces over and over again. In fact, we like to push the boat out a bit and try new things. Since our launch in 2019 we've welcomed a range of guest presenters to share their take on classical music, including Goldie, William Orbit, Sister Bliss from Faithless, Oscar-winning composer Anne Dudley, singer-songwriter Eddi Reader, garage pioneer DJ Spoony, Midge Ure, founder of the Kingdom Choir Karen Gibson, Nitin Sawhney and Doctor Who composer Segun Akinola. We've made special programmes about the music of the James Bond films, exploring how the natural world has inspired classical music, and the connection between football and classical music – and that's just for starters!

Mark Forrest is joined by a guest from the arts and entertainment world every weekday morning at 10.30am, chatting to musicians, directors, actors, comedians, chefs, broadcasters and more – and he speaks to an author every Thursday morning in the Scala Radio Book Club – so if you're a 'culture vulture', make a date with Mark! He also wants to you about your musical tastes, and plays your requests every weekday from midday.

We know that music from films, TV shows and video games can often be the 'entry point' for people to develop an interest in classical music, so you'll find 'Screen Time' with Charles Nove every weekday morning at 9am, providing the perfect complement to our Saturday film music show with Mark Kermode, and our weekly celebration of video games music, The Console with Luci Holland.

At the weekends, the music continues as Angellica Bell is joined by some of her well-known friends to talk about the classical music they love, how they discovered the genre and the how it makes them feel.

You can find Scala Radio broadcasting across the UK on DAB digital radio, smartphone or tablet using the free Scala App, smart speaker, on SKY TV channel 0216 and at scalaradio.co.uk. We look forward to welcoming you along – and we'd love to hear from you: email hello@scalaradio.co.uk any time and tell us what you'd like to hear more of!

A Soundtrack for Life is Scala Radio's first venture into the publishing world and is a snapshot of the type of music we love to play 24/7. We hope you enjoy it!

To find a playlist of the music featured in this book on Spotify, search for Scala Radio and click on the profile for the station.

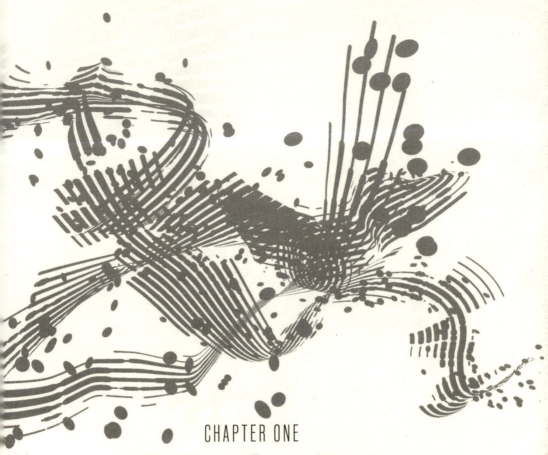

CHAPTER ONE

Through a Day

'Sunrise' Balázs Havasi

'Dawn' from Four Sea Interludes (*Peter Grimes*) Benjamin Britten

'Dressing for the Ball' from *Cinderella* Sergei Prokofiev

'Breakfast Machine' from *Pee-wee's Big Adventure* Danny Elfman

'Promenade' ('Walking the Dog') George Gershwin

'The Shrovetide Fair' from *Petrushka* Igor Stravinsky

'French Pastry' Richard Hayman

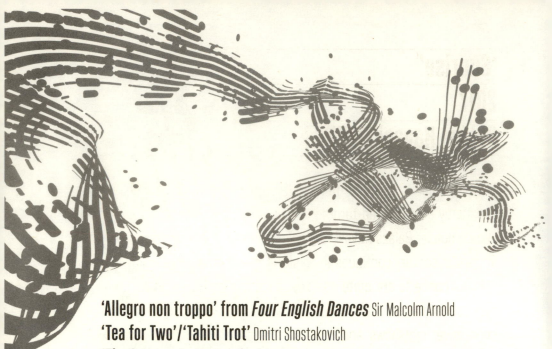

'Allegro non troppo' from *Four English Dances* Sir Malcolm Arnold

'Tea for Two'/'Tahiti Trot' Dmitri Shostakovich

'The Sorcerer's Apprentice' Paul Dukas

'Raindrop' Prelude Frédéric Chopin

TIME OUT & SLEEP

'Only in Sleep' Music by Ēriks Ešenvalds, words by Sara Teasdale

'Cumulonimbus' from *Sleep* Max Richter

'Largo' from Symphony No. 9 ('New World') Antonin Dvořák

'The Heart Asks Pleasure First' from *The Piano* Michael Nyman

'Reconciliation' from *Celeste: Farewell* Lena Raine

'Parce Mihi Domine' from *Officium* Jan Garbarek

'O Nata Lux' Thomas Tallis

'Nascence' from *Journey* Austin Wintory

'Locus iste' Anton Bruckner

Main theme from *Ocarina of Time: The Legend of Zelda* Koji Kondo

'Flight' Anoushka Shankar

'Nuvole Bianche' Ludovico Einaudi

'Ave Maria' Jaakko Mäntyjärvi

'Sunrise'
2017
Balázs Havasi (1975-)

Classical music is more magpie-like than some people believe, constantly evolving and turning in new directions. Hungarian pianist and composer Balázs Havasi is a good example of how music-making in the 21st century continues to be startling and innovative.

His concerts are quite an experience, closer in feel to an arena rock performance than a traditional recital, with big entrances, impressive lightshows and big screen projections, dance routines, plenty of drums and strings – and the piano centre-stage. He describes them as 'classical music meets a Las Vegas-style show' and while he has appeared at venues known for classical music concerts, among them Carnegie Hall in New York and the Sydney Opera House, he has also played Wembley Arena.

'Sunrise', the opening track from his album *Rebirth*, is a typically passionate piece. He flies up and down the keyboard – as befits a man who appears in the *Guinness World Records* as the fastest pianist in the world – before the strings and brass indicate the arrival of the Sun.

Havasi was classically trained at the Franz Liszt Academy of Music in Budapest and taught piano for some years, before turning towards a more diverse sound which features everything from Hungarian folk tunes to rock and world music. To produce this mix, he has worked with musicians as varied as Sir Karl Jenkins, Ronan Keating and Youssou N'Dour.

His goal is more than attracting a younger audience by making the piano cool. Havasi has described his vision as creating bridges between cultures, genres and art forms, but, as he points out, there is nothing new in this. One of his musical heroes is the 19th-century composer, conductor and pianist Franz Liszt whom he describes as the equivalent of the rock star of today. Certainly Liszt was a consummate showman and his concerts induced incredible hysteria among women in the audience along remarkably similar lines to those at Tom Jones's concerts; there was even a term for this frenzied behaviour: 'Lisztomania'. Havasi does not inspire the same kind of behaviour but his music is very deliberately a melting-pot offering food to all lovers of music.

WAKING UP

'Dawn' from Four Sea Interludes
(*Peter Grimes*)
1945
Benjamin Britten (1913-1976)

Various and vast, sublime in all its forms,
When lull'd by zephyrs, or when roused by storms,
Its colours changing, when from clouds and sun
Shades after shades upon the surface run;
Embrown'd and horrid now, and now serene,
In limpid blue, and evanescent green;
And oft the foggy banks on ocean lie,
Lift the fair sail, and cheat th'experienced eye.

This is an excerpt from George Crabbe's poem *The Borough* (1810), a series of 24 chapters that tell the story of the lives of various local people in an unnamed seaside town including a widow, a teacher and a clerk. This is part of number 22. It describes the moment Benjamin Britten tries to capture in the 'Dawn' section that comes just before the start of Act I in his 1945 opera *Peter Grimes*.

It's the beginning of the day in a 19th-century Suffolk coastal village, what Britten notes in the libretto as 'an everyday, grey seascape'. Clarinets, harp and violas depict the early morning wind on the North Sea (bassoon and brass instruments), with seagulls (violins and flutes) flying overhead. Within just a few bars, Britten manages to achieve a real sense of dawn breaking and the world coming to life.

Britten loved the sea and lived in Suffolk in the coastal town of Aldeburgh (coincidentally the birthplace of Crabbe) after returning to England in 1942 following three years in New York. The sea dominates the action throughout the opera, which tells the tragic story of Grimes, a fisherman, his young apprentices and the suspicious and unhelpful townsfolk. Crabbe's original poem is pretty harsh on Grimes, but Britten softened the character and while he hardly made him loveable, did raise the issue of how best to deal with life's outsiders.

While Britten's folk songs are very accessible, his operas are less immediately alluring; even the musicians who worked on the premiere of *Peter Grimes* were not initially convinced by it, although it became very successful. So while 'Dawn' and the other three interludes – 'Storm', 'Moonlight' and 'Sunday Morning' – can still provide unsettling moments, they are good places to start when first getting to know his work. Indeed, they are frequently performed together as a stand-alone quartet.

GETTING DRESSED

'Dressing for the Ball' from *Cinderella*
1945
Sergei Prokofiev (1891–1953)

There are two very different sections with characters getting dressed in the first act of Sergei Prokofiev's romantic ballet *Cinderella*. In the second, the old beggar woman whom Cinderella has welcomed in against her awful stepsisters' wishes turns out to be, of course, her fairy godmother. With the help of the fairies of spring, summer, autumn and winter, she helps Cinderella get ready for the ball and with a word of advice about the importance of keeping an eye on the clock, off she goes.

But before all this happens, we have seen the two sisters get ready in the 'Dressing for the ball' scene, a lighthearted, almost pantomime-like performance, which has echoes of the composer's music for his *Peter and the Wolf* written almost a decade before. Composed during the Second World War and premiered in 1945, the music has the same liveliness that permeates the rest of the popular ballet.

In fact this was a very deliberate sound that Prokofiev was trying to produce in order to give it a traditional feel; he had received numerous complaints from dancers for his previous work, the ballet music for *Romeo and Juliet*, which many had said was virtually undanceable. *Cinderella* was quite the opposite with plenty of comfortable set piece dances. He wanted, he said: 'to convey the poetic love between Cinderella and the Prince, the birth and flowing of feeling, the obstacles thrown in its path, the realisation of the dream.'

Cinderella was written specifically for one of the leading ballerinas at the time, Galina Ulanova (also one of those who had not taken kindly to his *Romeo and Juliet*). Prokofiev asked her what ballet she would like him to compose and this was her suggestion.

It was his last major work. Prokofiev became a victim of the post-war Soviet crackdown on artists who appeared not to conform entirely to fairly arbitrary creative limitations and his work fell seriously out of favour. Today, he is rightly regarded as one of the century's finest composers.

BREAKFAST

'Breakfast Machine' from
Pee-wee's Big Adventure
1985
Danny Elfman (1953-)

From the titles at the very beginning of the 1985 cult film *Pee-wee's Big Adventure*, the music lets you know that you're in for an hour and a half of screwball high jinks. Danny Elfman's score feels like it belongs alongside a *Looney Tunes* cartoon – and indeed he later wrote the theme tune for *The Simpsons* – with the music corresponding in a very unsubtle way to the action on screen.

So in the 'Breakfast Machine' scene, we watch Paul Reubens as Pee-wee Herman wake up, do some ludicrous exercises with tiny dumb-bells, then slide down the fireman's pole from his bedroom into the kitchen. Here he uses a Heath Robinson-type machine to make breakfast: a candle burns through a rope to drop an anvil to turn a toy ferris wheel which sends a table tennis ball through a chute which sets off a pterodactyl skeleton carrying two slices of bread which drop into a toaster as two toy guns smash two eggs into a frying pan and a small statue of a cherub drops his jar of pancake batter into another pan.

While all this is cooking . . . Pee-wee brushes his teeth.

Meanwhile, a T-rex skeleton squeezes some orange juice into a glass and another chute opens to launch dog food into his pet dog Speck's bowl. A moving statue of Abraham Lincoln flips a pancake (rather too hard, it lands on the ceiling next to three other failed attempts), a bell rings and, having weighed himself and been given a token by the machine advising him not to leave the house, Pee-wee rushes back into the kitchen to catch the toast as it hurtles out of the toaster. He sits down at the breakfast table and spreads butter onto his toast using an absurdly enormous knife. He then adds a generous serving of cereal to his cooked breakfast and tucks into it using an equally absurdly enormous fork. After a mouthful, he wipes his mouth with a napkin and leaves his home. It's five minutes of frantic Charlie Chaplinesque silliness.

Despite a strong slapstick element to the soundtrack, it's actually a very carefully created work, which includes various elements of homage and pastiche. Indeed, the whole film leans rather surprisingly on the 1948 Italian classic *The Bicycle Thieves*, which often tops Best Film Ever lists, as the plot hinges on Pee-wee's search for his stolen bike. 'Breakfast Machine' is a nod towards Italian composer Nino Rota's score for Federico Fellini's 1970 film *The Clowns*, and elsewhere in the film Elfman deliberately offers echoes of *Psycho* by Bernard Herrmann, who he acknowledges to be a major influence on his work, and the scene in *The Wizard of Oz* where we see the disagreeable Miss Gulch pedalling along on her bicycle.

The film was Elfman's big break into the world of film scores and enabled him to jump from being in a moderately successful pop group Oingo Boingo to the Hollywood big league. It was his first collaboration with director Tim Burton and, as well as working on hits such as *Good Will Hunting*, *Fifty Shades of Grey* and *Men in Black*, he has collaborated regularly with Burton on most of his films including *Batman*, *Edward Scissorhands*, *Charlie and the Chocolate Factory* and *Alice in Wonderland*.

DOG WALKING

'Promenade' ('Walking the Dog')
1937
George Gershwin (1898-1937)

There is no competition for the most stylish dog walking ever filmed. The award goes unanimously to Fred Astaire and Ginger Rogers in their seventh celluloid pairing *Shall We Dance*, the 1937 romantic comedy with a flirty score by George Gershwin to accompany them.

The plot of the film doesn't bear close examination, but Fred plays a ballet dancer who has a hankering for modern jazz dance. Ginger is a popular tap dancer and when they meet he makes a bit of a fool of himself. They then meet again on a steam liner while the great and the good aboard take their dogs for an evening constitutional. Fred tips one of the ship's staff to let him borrow his huge dog so that he can have an excuse to talk to Ginger, who is walking her tiny one. Gradually the other dog walkers move away, as does Ginger, who frankly gives him the cold shoulder.

The scene changes to the next morning when Ginger takes her dog out again from its on-board kennel. This time, Fred is fully prepared and appears bang on time, walking a dozen dogs of very varying sizes in a bid to impress her. This time there is a wry smile on her face and the two of them are soon promenading arm in arm on the deck, engaged in animated conversation.

They are accompanied throughout by one of Gershwin's wittiest and most elegant little melodies. Written for clarinettist Jimmy Dorsey, it's a perfect musical depiction of walking with a lovely solo opportunity for the clarinet against a perky background of piano (for which it was originally written), percussion and brass. There are some romantic strings thrown in for good measure. Gershwin was a dog lover himself and had numerous terriers including Tony, Tinker, and Bombo. In an odd quirk of fate, it's almost the only part of Gershwin's film score that has been published, the rest strangely unavailable.

Shall We Dance came hot on the heels of Gershwin's triumphant mix of classical and jazz, *Rhapsody in Blue*, but sadly he died soon after, receiving his Academy Award for work on the film posthumously.

SHOPPING

'The Shrovetide Fair' from *Petrushka*
1911
Igor Stravinsky (1882-1971)

Although ballets and operas often have slightly strange storylines, Igor Stravinsky's storyline for his ballet *Petrushka* is particularly unusual since it is a love triangle about three puppets that come to life.

The ballet opens at the Shrovetide Fair, the last celebration before the start of Lent, at an unspecified date in the 1830s. It is the Admiralty Square in St Petersburg where stallholders, dancers and entertainments are all contributing to an atmosphere of jollity, a Russian Mardi Gras. Among them is a showman who presents his puppet show, but one with a difference because once he plays his magical flute, the puppets suddenly become animated, Pinocchio-like. Petrushka – the Russian equivalent of our Punch – the Ballerina, and the Moor dance and then passions between them cause sparks . . .

Stravinsky not only wrote the music for the ballet, he also came up with the concept for it. He was at work on another piece when he said the clear image of a puppet that unexpectedly came to life flashed through his mind.

Audiences often found his work very challenging as he experimented with all kinds of musical techniques in unconventional ways. His collage technique, for example, in 'The Shrovetide Fair' section has been described as a musical mosaic, flitting around between various musical themes to give the impression of the shop-owners and activities all calling for attention. It is bright and colourful, the orchestra exactly capturing the excitement of a popular fair.

Petrushka was a great success when it opened in 1911 with the iconic Vaslav Nijinsky in the lead role. Audiences particularly warmed to its strongly Russian feel, as the folk tunes Stravinsky incorporated into the music were reflected in the traditional costumes and stage sets designed by Alexandre Benois. The French composer Claude Debussy was among those who loved it, writing to Stravinsky in April 1912 to tell him that Petrushka was full of 'a kind of sonorous magic'. Writing in the same year, Russian composer and critic Nikolai Myaskovsky said that 'Petrushka is life itself' and complimented the composer on its energy, freshness, merriment and 'reckless abandon'.

HOUSE CLEANING

'Allegro non troppo' from *Four English Dances*
1951
Sir Malcolm Arnold (1921-2006)

At a time in the middle of the 20th century when there was a trend towards composing dense and somewhat tuneless music, Sir Malcolm Arnold went quite the other way. Lively and very hummable, among his various symphonies, concertos and choral works is the remarkable *A Grand, Grand Overture for Three Vacuum Cleaners, One Floor Polisher, and Concert Band*, the main tinkety-tonk piano theme tune to the *St. Trinian's* films, and the soundtrack to *The Bridge on the River Kwai*, for which he won an Academy Award. He also wrote a harmonica concerto for the century's finest exponent of that instrument, Larry Adler.

'Allegro non troppo' comes from his sets of dances written in the early 1950s and inspired by the folk music of England, Ireland, Scotland, Wales and Cornwall. They all fall into the category of light music (see page 16) and are each only two or three minutes long, sprightly and catchy and the perfect background music while you're engaged in other household tasks. It was used for many years as the theme music for the BBC's *What the Papers Say* programme as well as a Sadler's Wells one-act ballet called *Solitaire*.

SNACK

'French Pastry'
1991
Richard Hayman (1920-2014)

Light music sits comfortably somewhere between classical and popular music. It's usually lively, tuneful and short. It was particularly popular in the 1940s and 1950s but has had a loyal following too over the last half century thanks to its entertaining feel-good factor. Think '633 Squadron' by Ron Goodwin, 'By The Sleepy Lagoon' by Eric Coates (the theme to *Desert Island Discs* on BBC Radio 4) or clarinettist Acker Bilk's 'Stranger on the Shore'.

'French Pastry' is a perfect example of an enjoyably light musical snack, 100 seconds of strings-led perky delight written by American composer and harmonica player Richard Hayman. He was closely associated with light music all his life, from early work in films to his major international harmonica hit in 1952, 'Ruby', which kickstarted a huge public interest in the instrument. Among the Hollywood films he helped to orchestrate was *Meet Me in St. Louis* (see page 99). For more than 30 years he also arranged music for the popular Boston Pops Orchestra in the US (the composer John Williams was principal conductor for many years and is its laureate conductor), which specialises in this form of music.

DINNER

'Tea for Two'/'Tahiti Trot'
1927
Dmitri Shostakovich (1906-1975)

It's not often composers get into major political trouble for producing light frothy pieces of music, but that's exactly what happened to poor Dmitri Shostakovich.

His 'Tahiti Trot' was his orchestration of the foxtrot duet 'Tea for Two', which first appeared as part of the 1925 musical *No, No, Nanette* by Vincent Youmans. It went on to become a major jazz standard covered by Duke Ellington and Benny Goodman, and sung by Doris Day and Ella Fitzgerald. Shostakovich's version starts with fine trumpets and dances round virtually the whole orchestra, giving many instruments solo chances to sparkle, such as the xylophone and woodblock, as well as a lovely flowing strings section.

In keeping with its frivolous nature, Shostakovich only pulled it together for a bet after his friend the conductor Nikolai Malko bet him 100 roubles he couldn't come up with a new orchestration from memory in less than an hour. Dmitri, whose time playing the piano in cinemas to accompany silent movies had given him a quick ear for thinking on the spot, won the bet and dedicated the result 'To dear Nikolai Andreevich Malko as a token of my best feelings'. He reused 'Tea for Two' in his ballet *The Golden Age* two years later.

But this frivolity was the problem. His four-minute version came only two years after the original and at a time when Soviet Russia was cracking down on music that it felt owed too much to capitalist Western society. 'Tahiti Trot' is very much that and it was part of the reason why the composer distanced himself from the piece for performance for many years and contributed to his spending some time in the artistic wilderness in that country.

WASHING-UP

'The Sorcerer's Apprentice'
1897
Paul Dukas (1865-1935)

There are, sadly, one-hit wonders in classical music too. French composer, teacher and critic Paul Dukas didn't help his cause by being hypercritical about his work and burning most of it, but his place in musical history is assured thanks to his *'L'apprenti sorcier'* or 'The Sorcerer's Apprentice'.

This 12-minute tone poem closely follows the storyline of a light ballad of the same name – *Der Zauberlehrling* – by the German writer Johann Wolfgang von Goethe (1749–1832). Enigmatic strings and flutes set the scene in the magician's den, as the apprentice discovers that the key to clearing up is to cast a spell (trumpets) over the broom (played by the bassoon). Unable to control its relentless march of water-gathering, he chops the broom (the cymbals representing an axe) which serves to multiply its efforts (the deep sound of the massive contrabassoon spiralling faster and faster). Only the magician's magic (the trumpets return) can bring the flood to a halt. Listen out too for the glockenspiel as it adds a sparkling supernatural touch to proceedings.

For many people the piece is closely associated with Mickey Mouse who starred as the apprentice in the exciting animated version in Walt Disney's *Fantasia* (1940). In fact this was the starting point for the entire *Fantasia* film. Disney initially envisaged just a short cartoon featuring Mickey and led by the famous conductor Leopold Stokowski. But the idea mushroomed into the hit multi-musical film still popular today, including 'The Dance of the Sugar Plum Fairy' (see page 149).

Sadly, Dukas grew to resent the success of 'The Sorcerer's Apprentice' at the expense of all his other work.

BATHTIME

'Raindrop' Prelude
1838
Frédéric Chopin (1810-1849)

It's the mark of the wide appeal of this six-minute piece by the Polish composer Frédéric Chopin that it sits just as happily in a James Bond film and a video game as well as a relaxing moment in your own home.

Officially called Prelude Op. 28, No. 15, it was named the 'Raindrop' by 19th-century German musician and Chopin enthusiast Hans von Bülow who took it upon himself to name all of the 24 pieces in the series, including 'The Night Moth', 'Suffocation' and 'Tolling Bells'. Chopin himself never really accepted the titles. 'Raindrop' is one of the longest of the set – some are very short indeed – and gets its title from the A-flat note that is constantly repeated, a sound that von Bülow and other listeners have likened to the sound of drops of rain. At first the 'drops' are gentle, gradually becoming heavier as a storm approaches, then quietly reappearing as it passes. Whether it really is supposed to be rain or not is up to the listener, but it's definitely ideal for moments when you want to unwind.

Another watery link comes from the story that Chopin wrote it during a stay in a Majorcan monastery where he was staying with his lover, the novelist George Sand, the pen name of Amantine Dupin. She recalled that while she was out with her son during a rainstorm, Chopin had daydreamed about the sound of raindrops falling regularly on a lake and been inspired to write the prelude, although he vigorously denied this was the inspiration.

Chopin's use of the term 'prelude' was innovative. Previously, preludes had been used, as their name suggests, as introductory works to something else. His were entirely individual and could therefore be played as stand-alone pieces, a tribute to the value of shorter works, or even perhaps be played in their entirety in a single performance.

It certainly appealed to Sir Hugo Drax who is playing it on the piano when he first meets Roger Moore's James Bond in the film *Moonraker*, as well as to the production team behind the advert for the video game *Halo 3* who used it as an atmospheric backdrop. It has also featured in the action film *Face/Off* (1997) and the Academy Award-winning *Shine* (1996) about the struggles of classical Australian pianist David Helfgott.

TIME OUT & SLEEP

'Only in Sleep'
2010
Music by Ēriks Ešenvalds (1977-),
words by Sara Teasdale (1884-1933)

Only in sleep I see their faces,
Children I played with when I was a child,
Louise comes back with her brown hair braided,
Annie with ringlets warm and wild.

Only in sleep Time is forgotten —
What may have come to them, who can know?
Yet we played last night as long ago,
And the doll-house stood at the turn of the stair.
The years had not sharpened their smooth round faces,
I met their eyes and found them mild —
Do they, too, dream of me, I wonder,
And for them am I too a child?

This exquisite sentimental poem was written by the American poet and Pulitzer Prize-winner Sara Teasdale and set to music in 2010 by the Latvian composer Ēriks Ešenvalds. It's a beautiful piece of choral music, simply done, with a lovely soprano soloist who hums as well as sings the nostalgic piece and drifts gently in and out of the music in a very dreamlike fashion. He has described his setting as 'like a very dear baby being swaddled in softest blanket'[1].

Ešenvalds has written operas and large-scale choral works, but he also specialises in these smaller songs which have a more intimate feel (interestingly, he says his first major muse was Whitney Houston). As well as 'Only in Sleep', he has set more than a dozen of Teasdale's poems to music, including 'Stars', which uses tuned crystal glasses and Tibetan singing bowls to depict the heavenly objects. He says he is drawn to the 'beauty and poignant simplicity of her poetry' and has similarly strong feelings about the power and importance of nature.

'Cumulonimbus' from *Sleep*
2015
Max Richter (1966-)

There aren't many pieces of music that can lull you softly to sleep and are still playing when you wake up the next morning. *Sleep* by English composer Max Richter is one of them because it comes in at an impressively hefty eight hours. It's ambient music at its most comprehensive, a testament to what Richter admits is one of his favourite activities.

Richter worked with neuroscientist David Eagleman to produce just the right kind of music that, in the best possible way, sends listeners off to sleep. The orchestration of piano, strings and electronic elements as well as some lyricless soprano vocals are carefully placed with peaks and dips to match the sleep cycle. These are not natural sounds in the sense of birdsong or wind in the trees, but they are tailor-made to be in natural harmony with your body. According to Richter it's 'an invitation to dream'.[2]

There are 31 pieces of varying lengths up to 30 minutes each that follow on seamlessly. *Sleep* starts with 'Dream 1 (before the wind blows it all away) and in an ideal listening world runs via 'Cassiopeia' (parts 1 to 6) and 'Sublunar' (parts 1 to 13) until it concludes a third of a day later with 'Dream 0 – till break of day' (part 31). 'Cumulonimbus' in two parts begins relatively early on, around the 15-minute mark. It feels like a long low hum and a little like taking a warm bath or watching the night sky lying on your back on the grass on a warm evening. There are changes of tempo and combinations of instruments in *Sleep*, and also some recurrent themes, but at no time is it startling and there are no high frequency sounds. Strangely, considering its length, it's never boring either.

Of course you don't need to listen to it while you're intent on sleep. Richter has talked about the need to pause in our current world where we sometimes appear to be always 'on'. It's as much about taking time out to relax, not just to snooze, with or without a pillow.

It's also been performed with a live audience several times overnight, with the audience provided with camp beds in which to sleep while they enjoy a communal listening experience. Nice for them, extremely demanding physically for the musicians.

'Largo' from Symphony No. 9 ('New World') 1893
Antonin Dvořák (1841-1904)

This is music about going on a journey. Packed by Neil Armstrong on Apollo 11, it was the first symphony on the Moon; it became hugely well known in the UK via the television advert for Hovis bread with the boy pushing his bicycle up a steep street; and it marked Czech composer Antonin Dvořák's delight in coming to America.

The 'Largo', the tender slow movement, is the second of four in the symphony written in 1893 and features the nostalgic sound of the cor anglais or English horn at its finest – hushed strings in the background. Dvořák chose the horn as he felt it was the closest sound to singing, specifically the voice of black composer and singer Harry Burleigh.

It was Burleigh who introduced Dvořák to African-American spirituals and while the Czech composer did not incorporate any actual traditional tunes into the symphony, they certainly inspired its writing. Words were added to the tune 30 years later by one of Dvořák's students, William Ames Fisher, and it became known as 'Goin' Home'. They fit so well that it is sometimes wrongly thought they were the source of the 'Largo' rather than the other way round.

'I am now satisfied,' he wrote the year he finished the 'Largo', 'that the future music of this country must be founded upon what are called negro [sic] melodies.'[3] Interestingly, this was the same period in which ragtime was becoming very popular (see page 299).

Dvořák loved America and the 'Largo' is partly a homage to Longfellow's poem *Hiawatha* and the wide open spaces it depicts. But he never lost his love of his homeland while he was working in his own New World and some of that longing can also be felt in the piece.

The 'Largo' found a new following in 2019 when Hovis brought back the original 1973 advert directed by Ridley Scott. Played at quite a sprightly speed, the music was recorded afresh by the Ashington Colliery Brass Band, which had performed on it the first time round.

'The Heart Asks Pleasure First'
from *The Piano*
1993
Michael Nyman (1944-)

In *The Piano* Holly Hunter does more than play the film's lead character, Ada, whose love for her piano survives an unhappy arranged marriage and emigration from her home in Scotland to New Zealand. She also plays the piano too.

Her ability as a pianist helped Hunter to secure the role since the piano in question is central to the film, a life support to Ada who is mute and communicates her feelings through her playing. English composer Michael Nyman, whose numerous early film scores with director Peter Greenaway include *The Draughtsman's Contract*, wrote half a dozen pieces for her to learn before filming began. It was so successful that when Hunter won the Best Actress Academy Award for her role, she thanked Nyman for composing music that helped her to create Ada's personality.

'The Heart Asks Pleasure First' is the best-known track from Nyman's score and is based on a Scottish tune by Robert Tannahill published in 1808 called 'Gloomy Winter's Noo Awa'. In the song, a lover talks about the joys of spring ('Come my lassie let us stray o'er Glennifer's sunny brae, And blythely spend the gowden day 'midst joys that never weary o'). But it adds that all the flowers in the world cannot bring joy unless a person is with their sweetheart. While Nyman had previously been stimulated by Baroque composers such as Purcell (see page 273), here he composed the soundtrack by trying to write the kind of music that a self-taught Scottish musician would produce for herself using inspiration from the music around her. 'I was composing a composer,'[4] said Nyman.

It's all written in Nyman's trademark style, building a soundscape with layers of repeating fragments, but with more of a melody than is usually associated with minimalism. In fact the film's director, Jane Campion, specifically said she did not want him to replicate the kind of structured score he had provided for Greenaway's films. Minimalism is often criticised for being cold and emotionless, but here it helps to build a feeling of passion as well as serving as Ada's escape from a harsh, unloving husband and environment.

Nyman renamed Tannahill's melody after a poem by 19th-century American poet Emily Dickinson, written around the same time *The Piano* was set, which focuses on what the heart wants most, pleasure. The soundtrack's sense of romance is in stark contrast to how it was mostly written: on a synthesiser plonked on a Black & Decker workbench while the builders were in.

Although Hunter's piano playing is good, it's not as good as Nyman's and for the official soundtrack he took over the recording duties himself.

'Reconciliation' from *Celeste: Farewell*
2018
Lena Raine (1984-)

In her youth, Lena Raine was a keen gamer. Among her favourites were *The Legend of Zelda*, the *Sonic* series and *Super Mario*. But while she enjoyed role-playing, what really interested her were the game soundtracks. The mix tapes that she put together were not hits from the pop music charts, but selections from the audio of some of her favourite games. After a fairly conventional musical upbringing and study at college, she found that this was the genre that excited her the most, composing music for imaginery gaming scenes.

Her CV includes music for *Minecraft* and the *Guild Wars 2* score, but her breakthrough work was for the big-selling *Celeste*. Notionally, this follows a young woman called Madeline as she makes her way up a mountain, but it also looks at the emotional and mental challenges she faces on her path too.

Raine worked on *Celeste* using synth musical software. Partly this is because she simply loved the sound and the freedom to play with her compositions on a trial-and-error basis, but also because it did not require a vast budget.

The soundtrack, nominated for a BAFTA, is incredibly varied. 'Reconciliation', written for the game's *Farewell* expansion, is one of the more tranquil pieces on which she plays piano using Spitfire Audio's Felt Piano software. The piano is Madeline's characteristic instrument, the guitar used for her companion Theo and the theremin – an electric instrument with antennas that you play by moving your hands rather than 'touching' it – for Mr Oshiro who lives on the mountain.

'Parce Mihi Domine' from *Officium*
1994
Jan Garbarek (1947-)
and the Hilliard Ensemble

Just as fusion food combinations sometimes throw up unexpectedly successful results, so the amalgamation of two quite separate genres can result in an unpredictably delicious recipe. On the menu here is a radical cocktail of medieval/Renaissance liturgical chant and 20th-century Nordic secular jazz saxophone.

Since Norwegian saxophonist Jan Garbarek and British early choral music specialists the Hilliard Ensemble released their 1994 album *Officium* it has sold on vinyl and CD of around the two million mark and been streamed millions more times. It is an amazingly fresh sound, mixing European church music from the 12th to the 16th centuries sung by countertenor David James, baritone Gordon Jones and tenors Rogers Covey-Crump and John Potter with sparingly restrained use of soprano and tenor saxophones. The recording was made in the suitably atmospheric acoustic of the Benedictine monastery of Propstei St. Gerold, Austria, rather than in a studio.

The opening track is the most 'modern', 'Parce Mihi Domine' by the early 16th-century Spanish composer Cristóbal de Morales. It manages to show off the clever improvisations of Garbarek, who has a long background in jazz, gliding and circling around the dazzling male vocals of the Hilliards. Neither dominates, they fold around each other, Garbarek's fluid sax acting almost as a fifth voice. And it's enchanting, the absolute definition of 'hauntingly beautiful'. It's so effective that when the 'Parce Mihi Domine' is sung later on the album without Garbarek, it feels like something is missing. Another standout is 'Beata Viscera' by the all-but anonymous Parisian composer Pérotin who lived in the 1200s, and here Garbarek's contribution is meaningful but more discreet.

Though the texts are in Latin, it doesn't feel like music for a church service, more the creation of a new musical language. It's the perfect riposte to people who argue that different periods and genres of music shouldn't be mixed. The fact that the sound can't be tidily pigeonholed is neither here nor there.

Officium was the first instalment of an ongoing musical experiment, coming out during a purple patch for medieval chant with the Benedictine monks of Santo Domingo de Silos in Spain releasing their bestselling *Chant* album (see page 260) the same year. Two later sequel albums by Garbarek and the Hilliard Ensemble, *Mnemosyne* and *Officium Novum*, appeared in 1999 and 2010, both featuring the same approach but using (slightly) more modern compositions. Together, they form a delicious three-course dinner.

'O Nata Lux'
1575
Thomas Tallis (c. 1505–1585)

For someone who is regarded as one of England's finest-ever composers, Thomas Tallis is something of a mystery. We're not at all sure when he was born or know about his family background, what he did in his youth (probably a chorister), what he looked like (there's no portrait of him by a contemporary), or when he wrote his masterpiece for 40 voices, 'Spem in alium'. He even signed his name Tallys.

What we do know is that he became a very successful composer at the royal Tudor court. He wrote and played for Henry VIII and his children Edward VI, Mary I and Elizabeth I, even though this was a torrid period for musicians as fluctuating religious rules had a significant effect on how church music was composed and performed. Tallis was a Roman Catholic but avoided becoming dangerously involved in liturgical storms.

The peak of his choral career came in 1575 when he was given the first patent to print and publish music by Elizabeth I and brought out *Cantiones sacrae*, a collection of 34 Renaissance songs called motets with fellow court-composer William Byrd (whose 'Ne Irascaris', written around the same time, will also delight those who enjoy this piece of Tallis). Among them was the remarkable, and remarkably short – just two minutes – 'O nata lux'.

The words for five voices come from a 10th-century hymn when the disciples have a vision of Jesus ('O nata lux de lumine'/'O Light born of Light') and call on him to accept the prayers of faithful followers. It's extremely soothing, with some lovely harmonies and almost inconspicuous dissonant clashes. While it doesn't need any ornamentation, the recording of it by the a cappella ensemble Voces8 includes a nicely judged saxophone.

After 1575, Tallis largely disappears back into the murk of history.

'Nascence' from *Journey*
2012
Austin Wintory (1984–)

Journey is a fascinating video game. The player embarks on a trip across a fictional Middle Eastern desert towards a distant mountain, a trek in which music is absolutely central to the story or, as the game's creator Jenova Chen describes it, 'the emotional North Star'.[5]

All the music is based around a single theme with individual instruments representing different characters from the opening track, 'Nascence', onwards. You as the main protagonist are signified by cello solos, older guides/ancestors by bass flutes (a really deep, mystical sound), and your online companions by the harp and viola. The game's composer Austin Wintory does this very cleverly so that it doesn't simply feel as if you are listening to the same thing over and over again. As you move through the game, the music becomes more complex.

Music is in fact the only way you can communicate with other players and objects as wordless 'singing' is the only action you can perform apart from walking and jumping. The music interactively follows your pilgrimage so the way you play the game – largely alone or travelling with others – alters your musical experience.

Wintory composed the music for a level, sent it in to the designers who added it to the prototype section and sent it back to him. He then played it and revised the music based on the gameplay. It was a long but fruitful process lasting three years in which he aimed for a universal sound rather than anything based on an individual culture. 'Nascence' feels a little like a sparsely romantic cello concerto with a South American lilt. Other tracks suggest a traditional Japanese and

36

Chinese influence. It is extremely mellow, in keeping with the idea that this is a game about emotions not about blowing things to smithereens. The score for *Journey* was nominated for a Grammy for Best Score Soundtrack for Visual Media, and it also won the BAFTA Games Original Music award in 2013.

'Locus iste'
1869
Anton Bruckner (1824-1896)

In daily life, Austrian composer Anton Bruckner was quite a modest and reserved man who loved playing the organ in his local church. But his nine symphonies were quite the opposite: bold and colourful, and bizarrely taken up gleefully by Adolf Hitler and the Nazis even though the composer shared none of their shameful ideology.

A world away from these longer works, Bruckner was devoutly religious and wrote many sacred choral works including numerous masses and settings of psalms. One of the most beautiful is his 'Locus iste'. It was written in 1869 to celebrate the dedication of a chapel at the newly finished Roman Catholic cathedral in Linz, Austria and is also sung in other churches on the annual anniversary of their foundation.

It begins 'Locus iste a Deo factus est', adapting lines from the books of Genesis and Exodus, 'This place was made by God'. It's an elegant celebration of an *inaestimabile sacramentum*, a priceless sacred space – though this doesn't have to be a building – for a soprano, alto, tenor and bass unaccompanied choir, with the bass voices to the fore. There's a gradual crescendo, but it's an ethereal swell rather than an overpowering one and the overriding sensation is one of serenity. Although it's marked to be sung moderately fast by Bruckner, it works best when it's slowed down a little.

Lovely to listen to at home and a favourite of choral groups of all standards, it's particularly restful if you hear it sung at a choral evensong in a church or cathedral, in the surroundings where it was meant to be savoured.

Main theme from *Ocarina of Time: The Legend of Zelda*
1998
Koji Kondo (1961-)

In the history of video game music 1984 is a key date. That was the year that Nintendo appointed its first musician dedicated to producing music for its games. Japanese composer Koji Kondo went on to become the company's flagship composer, responsible for the sound behind the ongoing evolution of *Super Mario* and the popular main theme of *The Legend of Zelda*.

His work on *Ocarina of Time: The Legend of Zelda* is regarded as particularly special. As in previous games in the series, the player controls the hero Link who has to solve various adventures as he battles against his enemy, the thief king Ganondorf. Players and locations have their own musical motifs and there were a number of game innovations, but the most fascinating introduction was the use of the controller as an instrument.

To progress through the levels, the player has to learn how to play a dozen tunes on the ocarina that Link receives early on in the game in order to solve problems. The ocarina – which appears early on in the title theme - is an ancient instrument, well over 10,000 years old, usually made of clay (though wood, plastic and other versions are also available) that is often likened to a flute-like sweet potato with holes in it. You blow through the main opening and adjust the sound by placing your fingers over the appropriate holes. Or, for *Ocarina of Time*, you use the button layout which matches that of the ocarina in the game, using the game stick to bend the sounds to vary them. Kondo said that he did not want the music to sound as if it was computer-generated, but like an actual instrument. As a direct result of the game, sales of ocarinas soared.

For the title theme of *Ocarina of Time*, the fifth in the series, instead of a speedy hullabaloo Kondo went for a relaxing ballad sound. Elsewhere, the score features other instruments with which players may also not be familiar, such as the Armenian duduk (a little like the oboe) and the resonating bamboo tubes of the Indonesian angklung. The soundtrack as a whole has taken on a new life outside sitting rooms, arranged regularly for orchestras, and spawning a whole genre of remixed versions. Maybe the game looks a little dated now, but the music is still going strong.

'Flight'
2013
Anoushka Shankar (1981-)

In the West, the sitar – a plucked stringed instrument like a guitar but with 18-20 strings – is strongly associated with the surname Shankar. For many years it was Ravi, but now it's Anoushka.

Like her father Ravi, Indian composer Anoushka is an expert sitar player and like him she has also ignored any tight musical boundaries to produce work that crosses borders between Western and Indian classical music. At the 2013 Grammy Awards, they were both nominated for separate albums in the Best World Music section (Ravi won with *The Living Room Sessions Part 1*) and since then she has continued to experiment, well beyond the creations of her father, adding layers of flamenco and electronica to her repertoire.

'Flight' comes from her 2013 album *Traces of You*, a collection inspired by the belief that everything and everybody leaves their mark on whatever they meet on their path. It's also a tribute to her father who died the previous year while she was working on it and features her half-sister, American singer-songwriter Norah Jones. 'Flight' shows off her superb sitar skills alongside the handpan, a member of the steelpan family, played by Austrian percussionist Manu Delago. The title alludes to the idea of the soul flying away from the body, particularly resonant given her father's death. It's by no means a sad piece, though, more a peaceful memorial of her intertwined personal and musical lives shared with Ravi.

With English composer Alex Heffes, Shankar also cowrote the score to the television adaption of Vikram Seth's novel *A Suitable Boy* in 2020 in a style she described as an Indian sound but with a global feel.

'Nuvole Bianche'
2004
Ludovico Einaudi (1955-)

From film scores (*Nomadland*) and television series (*This is England, 86*) to adverts (Santander, British Airways, the Sochi Olympics), the music of Italian composer Ludovico Einaudi has become a comfortingly constant presence in our lives. Sales and streams of his music are astronomical, his concerts always swiftly sold out. He is the sound of the century.

Classically trained, his work still has a classical flavour about it, but over the decades Einaudi has refined the sound to make it a genuine world music sound as befits a composer who counts among his influences Radiohead, Malian kora player Ballaké Sissoko, Philip Glass and master of the duduk Djivan Gasparyan from Armenia. Einaudi has talked about how he was attracted by the intimacy and immediacy of pop music in its widest sense of being 'popular', something without any musical divisions.

'Nuvole Bianche' (Italian for 'white clouds'; Einaudi often names his music after aspects of nature) first appeared on his 2004 album *Una Mattina* ('morning' in English), which was centred on the things he loved as he wrote: his family, his piano and his home, books and belongings, as well as the clouds and sunlight he saw out of his window. The track is an example of his signature pieces, which are introspective and reflective. There's an unadorned simplicity here. It's his own brand of 21st-century ambient minimalism, one with melodies that run easily through your head yet don't turn into annoying earworms. In this sense he is like his contemporary Michael Nyman (see page 29).

It's frankly music for the soul.

'Ave Maria'
1991
Jaakko Mäntyjärvi (1963-)

Many of the composers in this book have tried their hand at setting the Hail Mary prayer – better known as 'Ave Maria' – to music. One of the most successful modern efforts is by Finnish composer and choral singer Jaakko Mäntyjärvi who describes himself as an 'eclectic traditionalist'[6], working across genres but without hi-tech assistance.

He wrote it while he was teaching a choral composition course in Italy to demonstrate various musical techniques to his students at the end of course concert. Rather than add to the higher soprano-dominated Ave Marias, it stays generally in the lower and middle range, the basses heading for a low drone towards the end. It's clear and bright, and a refreshingly soothing jewel with real depth that will appeal to fans of Sir John Tavener (see page 63).

CHAPTER TWO
Events

BIRTHS
'Mi-A-Ou' from the *Dolly Suite* Gabriel Fauré
'Jimbo's Lullaby' from *Children's Corner* Claude Debussy

MARRIAGES
'Wedding Day at Troldhaugen' Edvard Grieg
'Wedding Cake' Camille Saint-Saëns
'Non più andrai' from *The Marriage of Figaro* Wolfgang Amadeus Mozart
'Meet the family' from *Pride and Prejudice* Carl Davis
'Danse de Fête' from *Coppélia* Léo Delibes

DEATHS

'The Lord bless you and keep you' John Rutter
The Infinite Ocean Oliver Davis
'Song for Athene' Sir John Tavener
'Fear No More the Heat o' the Sun' Gerald Finzi
'Agnus Dei' from *Eternal Light: A Requiem* Howard Goodall

MAJOR DATES

'A Red, Red Rose' Robert Burns
'Stranger in Paradise' Robert Wright and George Forrest
'Ubi Caritas et Amor' Paul Mealor
'The Last Rose of Summer' John Stevenson
'Songs My Mother Taught Me' Antonín Dvořák
String Quartet ('The Joke') Joseph Haydn
'Miserere' Gregorio Allegri
'Country Gardens' Percy Grainger
'Anthem' from *Us* Michael Abels
Music for the Royal Fireworks George Frideric Handel
'The Last Post' Alexis Ffrench
'A Mhaighdean Bhan Uasal' from *Brave* Patrick Doyle

CHRISTMAS

'Troika' from *Lieutenant Kijé* Sergei Prokofiev
'Somewhere in My Memory' from *Home Alone* John Williams
Overture from *The Muppet Christmas Carol* Paul Williams
O Magnum Mysterium Morten Lauridsen
'Andante quasi lento' from *Carol Symphony* Victor Hely-Hutchinson
'Have Yourself a Merry Little Christmas' Hugh Martin and Ralph Blane

BIRTHS

'Mi-A-Ou' from the *Dolly Suite*
1894
Gabriel Fauré (1845–1924)

French composer Gabriel Fauré enjoyed a flurry of creative output during an affair with his mistress Emma Bardac in the 1890s. One result was his 15-minute long *Dolly Suite*, right on trend at the time with the burst of pieces written for and about children, including *Children's Corner* by Claude Debussy (see page 48).

Composed mostly between 1894 and 1897, the *Dolly Suite* contains half a dozen short piano duets that Fauré wrote for and dedicated to Bardac's daughter Régina-Hélène. (There have been suggestions that she was his daughter, but this is probably not true.) Unusually for Fauré, he also gave the duets quirky names rather than his preferred dry classification titles.

For her first birthday he presented Régina-Hélène – nicknamed Dolly because she was quite small at birth – with the first piece, 'Berceuse' (later to find fame as the theme tune to the BBC's long-running radio programme *Listen With Mother*), and for her second he gave her 'Mi-A-Ou'. While the name suggests there's a cat-related anecdote behind the title, in fact it represents Régina-Hélène's attempts to pronounce her older brother Raoul's name. Nor is it actually quite the title Fauré gave it – he called it 'Miaou' – and his publisher simply decided it would look better with a couple of hyphens. It's a lively dancing tune and has been taken to depict both the toddler's efforts at pronunciation as well as her energetic brother's movements.

'Jimbo's Lullaby' from *Children's Corner*
1908
Claude Debussy (1862-1918)

French singer Emma Bardac (1862-1934) seemed to have a knack for producing children who inspired great composers to write music for them. One daughter, Régina-Hélène, was the dedicatee of the *Dolly Suite* (see page 47) by Bardac's lover Gabriel Fauré, and another, Claude-Emma, stirred Claude Debussy to produce *Children's Corner*. These six very different pieces for solo piano were written between 1906 and 1908 and dedicated to Bardac and Debussy's three-year-old daughter, whom he nicknamed Chouchou. 'To my dear little Chouchou,' he inscribed the manuscript, 'with tender apologies for what follows'.

The fact that the titles of all the pieces are in English – Debussy was a great Anglophile – may be a gesture to the family's English governess, Miss Gibbs. Like the *Dolly Suite*, *Children's Corner* was intended for children to listen to, rather than attempt to play.

Jimbo's Lullaby is the second piece, a gentle and witty plod for Chouchou's stuffed toy elephant after the pacy musical gymnastics of the first, *Doctor Gradus ad Parnassum*. Concentrating on the lower notes of the keyboard, it starts with the little elephant taking some tentative steps as bedtime approaches, marked by Debussy's instruction to musicians on the score to play it 'Soft and a little awkward'. It's a sleepy atmosphere with sections played pianissimo – very very quietly. Then he incorporates the tune of a famous French lullaby, 'Dodo, l'enfant do' which encourages an infant to fall asleep. Finally, the plodding returns as the baby falls gently asleep.

The piece is also a reference to a celebrated elephant of the day,

Jumbo, who came from the Sudan. He was a popular attraction at the zoo in Paris around the time Debussy was born, giving children rides on his back, before he was moved to London and eventually bought by the US showman P T Barnum and taken to America.

MARRIAGES

'Wedding Day at Troldhaugen'
1896
Edvard Grieg (1843-1907)

Troldhaugen, meaning 'Hill of the Trolls', was the name of Edvard Grieg's home just outside Bergen in Norway, and it was a place of great happiness for the Norwegian composer. Here in 1891 he built, and then worked in, an idyllic lakeside hut nearby. Whenever he finished work for the day, he left behind a message for intruders: 'If anyone should break in here, please leave the musical scores, since they have no value to anyone except Edvard Grieg.'

His equally much-loved house was also where he enjoyed a very happy marriage with his wife and professional soprano Nina Hagerup who also performed many of his songs in public. It was to her that he dedicated 'Wedding Day at Troldhaugen' as a gift on their 25th wedding anniversary.

The piece starts with a dance-like march, representing meeting guests. (There were hundreds at the actual anniversary party and the work was initially called 'The well-wishers are coming'.) This is followed by a quieter, thoughtful middle section before returning to the march. It's usually a six-minute piece, but there is a recording online of Grieg playing at a splendidly furious pace and knocking several minutes off that time.

'Wedding Day at Troldhaugen' is just one of 66 short pieces for piano that appeared in his *Lyric Pieces* series written between 1867 and 1901. Other highlights include the lively 'March of the Trolls' (which is reminiscent of what is perhaps his most famous work, 'In the Hall of the Mountain King'), a clever mimicking of birdsong in 'Little Bird', and 'Butterfly', which depicts the fluttering wings of a butterfly. The 'Berceuse' lullaby includes a tribute to the folk music of Norway about which Grieg was so passionate, and which brought him into contact with composers Frederick Delius and Percy Grainger who shared his interest (see page 162).

'Wedding Cake'
1885
Camille Saint-Saëns (1835-1921)

When Camille Saint-Saëns was weighing up what to give his piano duet partner and friend Caroline Montigny-Rémaury (1843–1913) as a wedding present, he settled on something much better than a toaster. Instead, the French composer – an infant prodigy whose pupils later in life included Gabriel Fauré (see pages 47 and 257) and Maurice Ravel (see page 271) – wrote her this charming and spirited waltz for piano and strings, which became known as the 'Wedding Cake'. Though it's hard to detect much specific cakiness in the piece, there is plenty of playful sparkle. The high spirits that animate it can also be heard in what has become Saint-Saëns' most famous work, composed the following year, *The Carnival of the Animals*.

'Non più andrai' from *The Marriage of Figaro* 1786
Wolfgang Amadeus Mozart (1756-1791)

It could happen to anybody. Your romance with the gardener's daughter is going really well when suddenly your boss catches the two of you together and decides to send you off to the army as a punishment.

That's the position poor Cherubino finds himself in at the end of Act I of Mozart's *The Marriage of Figaro*. The good news for us is that it heralds one of the most famous arias for a bass singer in opera, 'Non più andrai' ('You shall go no more'), a piece played by the Mozart character in the 1984 film *Amadeus*, one of Scala Radio presenter Simon Mayo's favourite movies of all time.

At this point in proceedings, Cherubino's boss, the Count Almaviva, is trying to stop the imminent marriage later that day between two more of his servants, Figaro and Susanna on whom he has set his own sights (there are lots of twists and turns before true love triumphs at the end). Figaro has a plan to help Cherubino – this being a comic opera it naturally involves dressing him up as a woman – but first takes the opportunity to poke a little fun at him.

Singing in a catchy but rather military manner, the marching effect backed up by the brass section of the orchestra, Figaro calls Cherubino an amorous butterfly but now there'll be no more romantic fluttering about at night. Instead, he paints a picture of the fresh-faced servant as a soldier in Seville with a moustache, weighed down with various weapons, and paid really poorly. Instead of dancing the fandango, he says, Cherubino will be marching through mud. Here's to glory in battle, he concludes, as they all march off stage.

Although the libretto, written by Lorenzo Da Ponte who also provided the words for Mozart's *Don Giovanni* (see page 133), is light and humorous, the original play by Pierre Beaumarchais on which it was based and that had premiered two years earlier, was far more controversial. To get the opera performed, Da Ponte omitted elements of the play's then shocking social revolutionary elements, for example a passage attacking the aristocracy was replaced by one about the inconstancy of women (which admittedly feels no better to our modern minds).

Sharp-eared listeners can hear Mozart sampling the tune to 'Non più andrai' in *Don Giovanni* where it is played onstage by a band and remarked upon as well known by the lead character's servant, Leporello.

'Meet the family'
from *Pride and Prejudice*
1995
Carl Davis (1936-)

The BBC's 1995 television production of *Pride and Prejudice* – Colin Firth's wet shirt and all – is universally acknowledged as the finest modern adaption of Jane Austen's classic novel. But it's almost impossible to think about it without the glorious soundtrack by American-born but longtime England-based Carl Davis, in particular the opening title music, also known as 'Meet the family'. The music immediately pulls us into the action: French horns and racing fortepiano accompany Mr Darcy and his friend Bingley as they gallop in and out of view – indicating that we're in for a lighthearted story about hunting and chasing – followed by Elizabeth Bennet admiring her surroundings (and the chaps on horses) and then skipping down a hill.

It's a very clever and elegant piece by a composer who is well versed in producing film and television soundtracks, among them *Cranford*, *The French Lieutenant's Woman* and *The Great Gatsby*, as well as for numerous silent movies. Although it includes a musical homage to a Beethoven scherzo that was popular around the time Austen wrote the novel, the music is deliberately reminiscent only of the period's music rather than an accurate recreation or imitation (it's not exactly pastiche and Davis understandably dislikes the term being applied to his music). So it's the sparkling fortepiano we hear playing the theme, a kind of evocative bridge between the more old-fashioned harpsichord and the modern piano. 'It's a funny mind game I play,'[1] says Davis.

The theme recurs throughout the series but in particular in what is the third movement in the *Pride and Prejudice Suite*, called 'Elizabeth and Darcy'. This version is much more romantic, more thoughtful and less horsey, with the string section to the fore. It's used when Darcy and Elizabeth go for a life-changing walk together . . .

Elsewhere there's lots of music-making in the series, including pieces by Handel and Haydn, Mozart's *The Marriage of Figaro* and *Don Giovanni* (see pages 53 and 133), as well as folk songs from around the time the book was published in 1813.

'Danse de Fête' from *Coppélia*
1870
Léo Delibes (1836-1891)

Coppélia is a lovely ballet but one that is unusual in several respects: it has a happy ending, it's essentially a comedy, and it has a strongly feminist approach throughout – most unusual for a 19th-century ballet.

The music by Léo Delibes accompanies a plot based on stories by E T A Hoffmann, the Prussian author who penned the original *The Nutcracker and the Mouse King* story (see page 149). Franz and Swanilda are two young villagers in love who plan to marry during a festival to inaugurate a new church bell. However, Franz becomes obsessed with a young woman named Coppélia who appears to be the daughter of local eccentric inventor Dr Coppélius. Strangely, all she does is sit very still reading all day on the balcony of the doctor's house.

Swanilda and her female friends take matters into their own hands. They break into the house to confront Coppélia and discover that she's a very lifelike mechanical doll made by the doctor. Swanilda plays a crafty trick on Coppélius and Franz (whom she has to rescue before he's forced to take part in a gruesome Frankenstein-like experiment), and love prevails; towards the end of Act III the happy couple perform their celebratory 'Danse de Fête' polka in the wedding scene. In the premiere performances in 1870, in an approach called *'en travestie'*, the character of Franz wasn't danced by a man, but by a woman, Eugénie Fiorce.

Throughout the plot, it's obvious that Swanilda is in charge and pushes the action forward. Almost as soon as the ballet begins she has a very complicated solo, and then dances throughout Act II, echoed in the additional stage time her female friends enjoy, unlike their male counterparts. And likewise, compared to Franz, who's a bit nice but dim, and Dr Coppélius, whose part is limited to being a laughable pantomime villain, Swanilda is a smart cookie. She's certainly a lot smarter and more practical than Coppélia who is a satire on the contemporary male idea of what the ideal young lady should be – lovely and silent.

Francesca Hayward, who danced the role for the Royal Ballet in a production in 2019, commented: 'She has so much more backbone than the average classical heroine . . . And it's so nice to play a girl with some control over her future. I always feel if she didn't want to marry Franz, she wouldn't.'[2]

DEATHS

'The Lord bless you and keep you'
1981
John Rutter (1945-)

John Rutter is one of our finest and most popular living choral composers, not least for the accessiblity of his pieces. While Rutter's work may not be as challenging as that of some other notable 20th-century composers, it is personal and emotional. As he himself commented: 'I happen not to believe in erecting needless barriers between composer and listener',[3] preferring to take the opportunity to touch people's hearts rather than satisfy professional critics.

Perhaps none of his works has touched people's hearts quite like 'The Lord bless you and keep you', chosen as part of their wedding music by the Duke and Duchess of Sussex for their nuptials in 2018. The piece is a gentle and sacred song about love, an expressive but restrained setting of a benediction also known as the Aaronic Blessing from the Bible (Numbers 6: 24–26):

> The Lord bless you and keep you:
> The Lord make His face to shine upon you,
> To shine upon you and be gracious, and be gracious unto you

There are various settings of it although a particularly lovely one for soprano and alto voices and sung by young choristers is a genuinely unforgettable experience.

But while it has become popular wedding music (it was also sung as part of the 100th birthday celebrations for the Queen Mother in 2000), it was in fact originally written by Rutter in 1981 for the memorial service of his music teacher, Edward Chapman, director of music at Highgate School in London (among Rutter's fellow pupils was Sir John Tavener who also wrote a memorable piece for the service, *Funeral Ikos*). When used for such sombre occasions, the second half of Rutter's text, verse 26, may provide additional comfort to the listeners:

> The Lord lift up the light
> Of His countenance upon you,
> And give you peace.

This is Rutter's farewell to his friend and mentor. It is only two and a half minutes long and is incredibly touching.

The Infinite Ocean
2018
Oliver Davis (1972-)

Music is capable of exploring every aspect of our life and Oliver Davis's *The Infinite Ocean*, the score for a new ballet choreographed by the Taiwanese-born American dancer and choreographer Edwaard Liang in 2018, focuses on the spiritual transition from our physical world to whatever waits for us beyond, a shift that Liang describes as 'the awakening'.

The piece is something of a tribute to Liang's friends who have died in recent years, stimulated by a message to him from one of them who wrote: 'I will see you on the other side of the infinite ocean.' Liang's instruction to his dancers was to think about who or what they would most like to see before they pass on, and what inspires them about what comes next – he has described *The Infinite Ocean* as a love letter to his father, the first person he would like to meet again. It is certainly not a work of despair.

As with all the best ballet music, Davis's work is a perfect match to what is a visually stunning piece of choreography against the backdrop of a huge sun. The dancers are paired in couples and in their duets they entwine around each other before peeling away. *The Infinite Ocean* is made up of six sections, which have a flowing cinematic feel and minimalist undertone. Starting with a powerfully emotional Baroque opening, there is a particular emphasis on the solo violin throughout, although the concept of transition, which is central to the ballet, is reflected in the changing moods of the pieces, with a calming Pas de Deux and plenty of work for brass, percussion and woodwind.

The Infinite Ocean was written on commission for the San Francisco Ballet, but choreographers have also successfully mined much of Davis's other work from previous albums including *Flight*, *Dance* and *Liberty*. His partnership with Liang is an ongoing one and includes the 2019 collaboration *Constant Light*.

'Song for Athene'
1993
Sir John Tavener (1944-2013)

Alleluia. May flights of angels sing thee to thy rest.

Remember me O lord, when you come into your kingdom.

Give rest O Lord to your handmaid, who has fallen asleep.

The first time most people heard these words sung was at the funeral in 1977 of Diana, Princess of Wales, as eight Welsh guardsmen pall-bearers carried her coffin out of Westminster Abbey at the end of the service. Written by English composer Sir John Tavener four years earlier, it formed part of a uniquely eclectic selection of music played throughout the funeral. Put together by Dr Martin Neary, the organist at Westminster Abbey and musical director for the service, it ranged from traditional hymns and requiem selections to Elton John's reworking of 'Candle in the Wind'.

Tavener's piece has something of a hauntingly ancient feel, almost otherwordly, about it, as does much of the composer's work. He once remarked that there were a lot of artists who were good at leading us into hell. 'I would rather someone would show me the way to paradise,'[4] he said.

A hypnotic low bass note drone is sung constantly underneath repeating Alleluias and a beautiful text selection combining quotations from William Shakespeare's play *Hamlet* and the funeral service of the Eastern Orthodox Church (Tavener had converted several years previously to the Russian Orthodox faith). Gradually the seven-minute elegy increases in volume to an intense climax which filled the remarkable space of the Abbey. It is sung, sometimes almost inaudibly, by a standard soprano, alto, tenor, and bass choir, unaccompanied by instruments.

The combination of texts was commissioned by Tavener and written by an orthodox nun, Marina Sharf, known as Mother Thekla. She was based in Whitby and was something of a spiritual mentor to him. Tavener composed the music after another funeral service, that of his Greek friend Athene Hariades, who died in a cycling accident. He said the melody came to him in the graveyard after the service and he wrote it down immediately on returning home.

'Fear No More the Heat o' the Sun'
1942
Gerald Finzi (1901-1956),
performed by Amy Dickson (1982-)

The idea that the saxophone is the ideal instrument for playing musical settings of Shakespeare's poems might raise eyebrows in some traditionally minded quarters. Nevertheless, the happy combination of Australian saxophonist Amy Dickson and self-educated British composer Gerald Finzi makes for a delightful sound.

Finzi enjoyed the quiet of country life in Wiltshire where he could grow apples and build up an impressive home library. In the 1930s and 1940s, under the general title *Let Us Garlands Bring*, he put together a cycle of five songs by Shakespeare from his plays *Twelfth Night*, *The Two Gentlemen of Verona*, *As You Like It* and *Cymbeline*. The songs vary in subject matter but the Bard's plays provided him with 'Fear No More the Heat o' the Sun', a placid musing on the passing of time and the inevitability of ageing and all that it entails. It starts:

> Fear no more the heat o' the sun
> Nor the furious winter's rages;
> Thou thy worldly task hast done

While Finzi's intention was that it be sung – he was a wide reader and had a deep love of English literature, especially the poems of Thomas Hardy – the song actually works very well in the beautiful instrumental version performed by Dickson. She has worked hard to raise the standing of the saxophone as an orchestral instrument and has consequently introduced a whole new generation of listeners to classical music. Interestingly, Dickson has talked about how she sometimes feels as if she is singing while she plays, and here she certainly brings out the lyricism in Finzi's song.

'Agnus Dei' from *Eternal Light: A Requiem*
2008
Howard Goodall (1958-)

There are many musical settings of the Requiem Mass used at funerals and memorial services going back centuries and some have become so popular that they are now performed in concerts in their own right. Although the 20th century saw some change in approach with many war-themed requiems produced by contemporary composers, it's essentially a Catholic Mass, written entirely in Latin and, unsurprisingly, rather sombre.

Howard Goodall's 21st-century take on the genre, *Eternal Light: A Requiem*, differs in various ways. For a start, it was commissioned uniquely as a choral-orchestral-dance piece to be performed by the Rambert Dance Company in 2008. Since Goodall's music was to be danced, he was particularly intrigued by how he might be able to indicate the concept of the flight of the soul.

Goodall – whose work for British television includes the themes to *The Vicar of Dibley* and *Blackadder* – is evangelical about making classical music available to everyone and has presented various television series about it since 2013. So it made sense for him to decide to move away from the more severe parts of the Requiem, which range bleakly over sin, judgement and everlasting damnation. In terms of the lyrics, this meant pulling back from the feelings of loss and concentrating on offering 'solace for the living that mourn'. His reinterpretation reduces the size of the traditional Latin Mass text and incorporates appropriate lines of poetry in English from the last 500 years. Some of it is sacred, some secular, reflecting his hope that those who are religious as well as those who are not can each find something that speaks to them.

'Agnus Dei' (Lamb of God) is actually one of the parts where Goodall has left all the words in Latin:

> Agnus Dei, qui tollis peccata mundi, miserere nobis
> Agnus Dei, qui tollis peccata mundi, dona eis requiem
> (*Lamb of God, that takest away the sins of the world, have*
> *mercy on us*
> *Lamb of God, that takest away the sins of the world, grant*
> *them rest*)

The 'Agnus Dei' section was the first part of the requiem that Goodall wrote. The five-minute piece comes towards the end of *Eternal Light* and features a tenor or baritone soloist. It's a touching and quite catchy composition that feels reflective and encouraging rather than gloomy. As Goodall says: 'Music's ability to transport us from the everyday, to evoke some other, peaceful place is one way we can offer any crumb of comfort.'[5]

MAJOR DATES

BURNS NIGHT
'A Red, Red Rose'
1794
Words by Robert Burns (1759-1796),
performed by Eddi Reader (1959-)

> O my Luve is like a red, red rose
> That's newly sprung in June;
> O my Luve is like the melody
> That's sweetly played in tune.

The Scottish writer Robert Burns has long been celebrated for his own original poems, but he was also a keen collector of folk songs, saving more than 300 for posterity. One of his most popular romantic works was 'A Red, Red Rose', which he pulled together from various other ballads.

In four four-line verses, the singer emphasises his everlasting love for his sweetheart, a love that will last until the seas run dry and rocks melt in the sun. These ideas had appeared in other printed collections in previous centuries but, like Shakespeare, his genius lay partly in his ability to synthesise these disparate elements. Burns described it in a letter to a friend as 'the simple and the wild',[6] yet not so simple that it prevented Bob Dylan from picking it as the lyrics that have had the biggest impact on his own life.

Various musicians put the words to music, but the version that is now the most popular is the 18th-century tune 'Low down in the Broom' which Burns knew but never suggested using himself. Scottish tenor Kenneth McKellar (1927–2010) recorded a popular version in the 1960s but Eddi Reader, formerly of Fairground Attraction, has put her own imprint on it for a new generation. As a young girl she had no time for his work, but has changed her opinion entirely, describing him now as 'a spokesman for the glorious in the ordinary, the sublime in the mundane.'[6]

Reader presented a month-long series on Scala Radio in which she celebrated traditional folk music of the British Isles and explored the intersection between folk and classical music. In the gentle acoustic version for 'My Love is Like a Red, Red Rose', which appears on her 2003 album *Sings the Songs of Robert Burns*, she swaps in 'bonnie lad' for 'bonnie lass'.

It's not entirely clear what specific red, red rose Burns had in mind, although one theory is that it is the wild dog rose, which does indeed flower in June.

VALENTINE'S DAY

'Stranger in Paradise'
1953
Robert Wright (1914-2005)
and George Forrest (1915-1999)

To paraphrase the 17th-century author of *Paradise Lost*, poet John Milton: to borrow and better in the borrowing is no plagiary. There are musical crossover quotes in the most unexpected places, from Little Mix's 'Little Me' and S Club 7's 'Natural', which both reuse Gabriel Fauré's 'Pavane', to the Pet Shop Boys and the Village People mirroring Johann Pachelbel's 'Canon in D', so popular these days at weddings.

One of the most successful musical adaptions is the 1953 musical *Kismet*. The lyrics and music are by Robert Wright and George Forrest who had already given Norwegian composer Edvard Grieg's music the same refurbishment in the 1944 operetta *Song of Norway*. For *Kismet*, they turned to Russian composer Alexander Borodin (1833-1887) for inspiration.

The Arabian Nights rom-com story follows the adventures of a slightly disreputable beggar-poet and his beautiful daughter Marsinah who falls in love with the young Caliph in Baghdad. Wright and Forrest mined numerous of Borodin's works for a dozen of the songs, including his Symphonies 1 and 2, 'In the Steppes of Central Asia', and his String Quartet No. 2 (for the lovely 'And This is My Beloved' as well as the jaunty 'Baubles, Bangles and Beads').

What became the biggest stand-alone success – a number 1 hit in the UK for Tony Bennett but also covered by Bing Crosby – was 'Stranger in Paradise'. This was taken from the 'Polovtsian Dances' section of Borodin's opera *Prince Igor* where it is called, rather winningly, the 'Gliding Dance of the Maidens'. It's a lovers' duet between the Caliph and Marsinah (sung in the successful MGM 1955 film by Vic Damone and Anne Blyth). The song comes at the moment when they meet for the first time in a lovely garden. They describe their almost mystical feelings for each other as they fall in love in what to them now feels like paradise. The original is as beautiful a piece of music as the song is gorgeously romantic.

Less well known is that in 1940, more than a decade before *Kismet* hit Broadway, clarinettist Artie Shaw and his orchestra also recorded a version of the same piece of music by Borodin, with no attribution and different lyrics sung by Pauline Byrne, under the name 'My Fantasy'.

ST DAVID'S DAY

'Ubi Caritas et Amor'
2011
Paul Mealor (1975-)

The wedding of Prince William and Kate Middleton in 2011 brought several pieces of music to a wider public audience (see Stromness page 213). It also propelled Welsh composer Paul Mealor to international fame.

Kate Middleton had heard an amateur choir sing his song 'Now Sleeps the Crimson Petal', using words from the Alfred Lord Tennyson poem of the same name and enjoyed it so much she asked if it could be used during her marriage service. Mealor was delighted – he has described it as 'the biggest gig of any composer's life'[7] – but suggested swapping the secular Tennyson words for the sacred Latin text of 'Ubi Caritas'. This is traditionally associated with Maundy Thursday services and is very much about the central part of love in our lives. It's one of the oldest antiphons, or hymns, dating back more than 1,500 years. It's also quite long, but has been reduced over the centuries. Mealor used only the first verse:

> Ubi caritas et amor, Deus ibi est.
> Congregavit nos in unum Christi amor.
> Exseultemus et in ipso jucundermur
> Timeamus, et amemus Deum vivum.
> Et ex corde diligamus nos sincere.

Where charity and love are, God is there.

Christ's love has gathered us into one.

Let us rejoice in Him and be glad.

Let us fear, and let us love the living God.

And may we love each other with a sincere heart.

Mealor's setting for unaccompanied choir, slightly changed from his original piece, is calming and reflective but still retains a feeling of traditional chant with a recognisably modern touch (it was used on the BBC Two sitcom *Rev*). It bears comparison with the work of Morten Lauridsen (see page 97) and is also an echo of the way Elton John adapted 'Candle in the Wind' for the funeral of William's mother, Diana, Princess of Wales.

Although he has written in various genres, much of Mealor's work is choral. As well as opera he also wrote the song 'Wherever You Are', sung by the Military Wives Choir, which was the Christmas number one the same year as the royal wedding. He also went on to write music for Queen Elizabeth II's Diamond Jubilee celebrations.

ST PATRICK'S DAY

'The Last Rose of Summer'
1813
Words by Thomas Moore (1779-1852),
music by John Stevenson (1761-1833)

'Tis the last rose of summer
Left blooming alone;
All her lovely companions
Are faded and gone;
No flower of her kindred,
No rose-bud is nigh,
To reflect back her blushes,
Or give sigh for sigh.

I'll not leave thee, thou lone one!
To pine on the stem;
Since the lovely are sleeping.
Go, sleep thou with them.
Thus kindly I scatter
Thy leaves o'er the bed,
Where thy mates of the garden
Lie scentless and dead.

So soon may I follow,
When friendships decay,

And from Love's shining circle
The gems drop away.
When true hearts lie withered,
And fond ones are flown,
Oh! who would inhabit
This bleak world alone?

There are hits and there are hits. In 1805, Irish poet Thomas Moore was inspired by a pink rose called 'Old Blush' to add lyrics to a beautiful traditional Irish folk tune called 'Aislean an Oigfear' ('The Young Man's Dream'). He cannot in his wildest dreams have imagined then how successful it would be.

The song was published in his multi-volume work *Irish Melodies*. This brought more than 120 Irish folk songs with piano arrangements by Irish composer John Stevenson to a highly appreciative international audience. 'The Last Rose of Summer' in particular, despite its rather melancholic lyrics, was a monster success throughout Europe, and in the US alone 1.5 million copies of the sheet music were sold in the 19th century.

Since then it's been covered by everybody from Nina Simone to Charlotte Church, and used by classical composers, including Ludwig van Beethoven, Felix Mendelssohn and Benjamin Britten. It also has a long history in films from playing a key part in the 1941 Academy Award-winning *Here Comes Mr Jordan*, to the beginning and end of *The Ladykillers* (1955), and the 2020 adaption of Jane Austen's novel *Emma*. It also appears in the 2017 film *Three Billboards Outside Ebbing, Missouri*, sung by American soprano Renée Fleming in a version composed by German composer Friedrich von Flotow (1812–1883) for his opera *Martha*.

MOTHER'S DAY

'Songs My Mother Taught Me'
1880
Antonín Dvořák (1841-1904)

Passionate patriot Antonín Dvořák loved the traditional folk songs of his Czech homeland and used many of these tunes in his music. Although best known for his symphonies and lively *Slavonic Dances*, he also wrote several popular song cycles. The seven that make up his *Gypsy Songs*, written in 1880, are a romantic tribute to the wandering life of the gypsy, as well as an affirmation of the importance of Czech self-determination. Among them is 'Songs My Mother Taught Me' (*Když mne stará matka zpívat učívala*).

This is a warmly nostalgic little piece that is typical of the strong emotions that pour from his work. The music is set to a text by Czech poet Adolf Heyduk and was written specifically for Czech operatic tenor Gustav Walter with piano accompaniment. In English, the singer remembers the songs sung by their mother long ago, often with a tear in her eye. Now, the singer is teaching those same songs to their own children, and the memories cause the tears to flow again as the music is passed down the generations. It's a real 'not a dry eye in the house' piece.

There are many arrangements of this romantic happy–sad piece, including for piano quartet, trumpet, violin and harp. It's also been a popular standard for soloists, among them Paul Robeson and Renée Fleming. One of the loveliest is by cellist Yo-Yo Ma.

APRIL FOOL'S DAY

String Quartet ('The Joke')
1781
Joseph Haydn (1732-1809)

Classical composers are not known for their wacky pranks, but the Austrian Franz Joseph Haydn is an exception. Kicked out of a choir as a teenager for cutting off a fellow chorister's pigtail, Haydn was known for his jovial approach to life as well as being one of the most famous composers of his day. 'Since God has given me a cheerful heart,' he said, 'He will forgive me for serving Him cheerfully.'

His love of mild mischief extended to his compositions. As well as some fairly arcane musical in-jokes, Haydn also provided his audiences with plenty of less subtle messing about including:

* during his Symphony No. 45 (known as the 'Farewell Symphony') the musicians gradually get up one by one and leave the platform until only two violinists remain.

* the music appears to stop near the end of his Symphony No. 90, giving the audience the cue to start clapping, only for it to start up again.

* a loud bass fart noise played by the bassoon in the increasingly quiet section of the 2nd Movement in his 93rd Symphony.

* a quiet section in the 2nd movement of his 94th Symphony (dubbed the 'Surprise Symphony') is suddenly broken by a loud chord before resuming as if nothing had happened.

Haydn's 1781 String Quartet, nicknamed 'The Joke', is similarly playful. The final section has a series of increasingly long pauses, each one suggesting that the piece is over before carrying on. And then it suddenly stops. It is maybe not a conventional sidesplitting gag, but it is a surprisingly funny listen and apparently had his 18th-century audiences in stitches.

EASTER

'Miserere'
c. 1630
Gregorio Allegri (1582-1652)

This is simply one of the most beautiful pieces of music ever written.

At some point during the 1630s, Italian singer and composer Gregorio Allegri set the words of Psalm 51 to music for candlelit Easter matins services in the Sistine Chapel in Rome. *Miserere mei, Deus*, it begins, 'Have mercy on me, God', going on to ask for forgiveness for sin and the chance to start a new, upright life. Gradually, the candles are blown out until only one remains.

The work has been wrapped in various stories of dubious authenticity – that anybody who copied it would be excommunicated, that a young Mozart was the first to smuggle the music out in his head and then wrote it down – but interestingly the piece we hear today is quite different from how it would have sounded almost 400 years ago. Written initially for nine voices split into two sections and then passed down orally between singers, it's a deceptively simple piece with a repeating theme interrupted by plainsong. Allegri's original version allowed the singers room to add their own embellishments, known as *abbellimenti* (it's these and the general technique that were kept hush-hush rather than the actual composition, which was well known before Mozart 'uncovered' it).

The most famous element of the 12-minute piece is the very high note that comes several times during a performance, a challenging top C, sung either by a young treble chorister or a soprano. But Allegri didn't write it in. Somewhere along the line it became a central element, probably due to a printing error when Felix Mendelssohn transcribed it in 1831.

Whatever the truth of its history, this sublime work is now one of the most popular choral works. There's a marvellously atmospheric 1964 recording with boy treble Roy Goodman hitting the high notes with the Choir of King's College, Cambridge. The Sixteen is among recent choirs that have also gone back to the original, without that C.

ST GEORGE'S DAY

'Country Gardens'
2018
Percy Grainger (1882-1961)

The musical interests of Australian-born composer and pianist Percy Grainger could scarcely have had a wider span. In the last decade of his life, well ahead of the arrival of synthesisers, he became fascinated by the idea of experimental electronic music and what he called 'free machines' which would play music without human intervention.

However, he was also fascinated by traditional English folk music as a teenager. In his twenties Grainger became one of the small band of early 20th-century musicians led by Cecil Sharp who collected examples from around England to prevent their disappearance (see 'On Hearing the First Cuckoo in Spring', page 162). Grainger spent five years collecting around 350 songs using a phonograph, an early record player that recorded sound on wax cylinders, and which you can listen to on the British Library's website.

One of those collected by Sharp was gathered in 1906 from a well-known Oxford-based concertina player and Morris dancer, William Kimber. Grainger took this simple Morris dance tune, which dates back at least as far as the early 18th century, and in 1918 as a birthday present for his mother turned it into the lively 'Country Gardens' for piano. Online you can hear him playing it, really quite fast.

A remarkable concert pianist and a notable composer himself, Grainger was adept at producing similar jaunty short pieces such as 'Handel in the Strand', 'Shepherd's Hey', and 'Molly on the Shore'. But he became tired of his close association with 'Country Gardens', despite the fact that he did very well indeed from its royalties and that it was very popular; jazz giant Charlie Parker even enjoyed sprinkling bits of it into his live performances. Grainger made various new, slightly mocking, orchestrations of it including one with deliberately wrong notes, 'so you can think of turnips as I play it'[8] he explained.

In the 1960s, lyricist Robert Jordan added lyrics that listed how many sweet flowers grow in an English country (beat) garden. It also listed some birds including the bobolink and tanager which you're most unlikely to find there. Sung by American Jimmie Rodgers it became a big hit and inspired covers from Nana Mouskouri to Rowlf and Fozzie from the Muppets. American Allan Sherman messed about weirdly with its lyrics and turned it into 'Here's to the Crabgrass', an account of suburban American life. Readers may also remember some less fragrant adaptations from schooldays . . .

HALLOWE'EN

'Anthem' from *Us*
2019
Michael Abels (1962-)

Though not technically set on Hallowe'en, the 2019 horror movie *Us* has a soundtrack by American composer Michael Abels that will have your nerves jangling. Imagine Bernard Herrmann's famous music for *Pyscho* on top of John Williams's score for *Jaws* then ratchet it up several notches. Mark Kermode, presenter of Scala Radio's weekly film music show, also likens it to the devilish 'Ave Satani' chant from Jerry Goldsmith's score to the movie *The Omen*.

The film tells the story of the sudden appearance of not entirely pleasant doppelgängers who pop up in California. 'Anthem', which appears over the opening credits, is one of the most chilling tracks. Director Jordan Peele, with whom Abels worked on a previous horror film *Get Out* (2017), asked for 'gospel horror' and Abels certainly came up with the goods. 'Anthem' features a choir of 30 people, a third of which are children, singing nonsense lyrics.

On the page, 'Do mi na vi ri fo sa ci' looks fairly innocuous, but it's performed in a kind of evil choral chant style against a background of increasingly spiky violins, drum beats and chimes, ending in a worryingly understated climax. 'Anthem' represents the doppelgängers' anger and hints at them marching forward with their very upsetting plans. Though the lyrics sound a bit like Latin, they are deliberately incomprehensible so that there are no clues about what's coming up later. Abels checked his constructed gibberish was meaningless by Googling anything that looked potentially genuine. For *Get Out*, he adopted a similar approach but used Swahili, which did offer some clues to those who understand the language. The 'Anthem' theme reappears regularly throughout the action.

Since the film focuses on unusual duality, Abels was encouraged to use unfamiliar combinations elsewhere in the score. Among these were the violin with the cimbalom (a hammered dulcimer), the didgeridoo with a kalimba (a kind of handheld African glockenspiel) and the berimbau (a Brazilian single-string violin).

The music was produced in an interesting way. Abels read the script before shooting started and then began composing, passing on sections as they were written. He was then shown rough cuts of how his work was being placed and used this to gauge what was required for future shots.

GUY FAWKES DAY

Music for the Royal Fireworks
1749
George Frideric Handel (1685-1759)

The end of the eight-year War of the Austrian Succession between the English and the French provided the opportunity for King George II to throw a massive party in Green Park, London, complete with a huge fireworks display. The monarch turned to the leading composer of the day, George Frideric Handel, who had written his coronation anthem still used today, to provide the music for the event.

Handel came up with something quite spectacular for the celebrations on 27 April 1749, a suite in six movements for a whopper of a wind band – 12 bassoons and contrabassoon, 24 oboes, 14 trumpets and horns, a serpent (a kind of snakelike tuba), three pairs of kettledrums and numerous side drums. Rather against his will, Handel had to take the string section out when the king casually mentioned that he 'hoped there would be no fidles' but quietly put it back in for the first public performance.

The music is jaunty and catchy – one of Handel's trademarks – beginning with a stately overture with exciting drumrolls and fanfare flourishes, then moving into lively dances. Each movement has a name, some indicating the reason for the composition's commission, so the third is called 'The Peace' and the fourth 'The Rejoicing'. The latter is the best-known section with trumpets and percussion in full festive mood. 'What the English like,' said Handel, 'is something that they can beat time to, something that hits them straight on the drum of the ear.'[9]

The music – which was performed in the intervals between fireworks - was immediately acclaimed as a masterpiece, although the firework display was a mixed success. Several onlookers and soldiers were hit by fireworks, one of the park's pavilions burned down, and the cloudy rainy weather was a pain. Yet the event still attracted around 10,000 paying customers whose arrival caused a massive traffic jam on London Bridge.

In June 2002 the suite was performed for Queen Elizabeth II's Golden Jubilee in the gardens of Buckingham Palace. And the fireworks went off without a hitch.

REMEMBRANCE SUNDAY

'The Last Post'
2018
Alexis Ffrench (1970–)

'The Last Post' bugle call dates back to at least the 17th century when it was used as a marker for the last of the day's inspections of the army's sentry posts. During battle, it also indicated the conclusion of warfare for the day.

Gradually, although particularly after the end of the First World War, it has become a central element in military funerals and Remembrance services, a respectfully symbolic conclusion to a soldier's life and duty. Originally lasting around 45 seconds, it has become lengthier as more weight is given to the emotional rather than formal side of the playing, including extended pauses and notes held for longer, rather than through musical additions. The arrangement by British composer and pianist Alexis Ffrench, which appears on his 2018 album *Evolution*, runs to nearly three and a half minutes.

Scala Radio presenter and Composer in Residence Ffrench is committed to making classical music more accessible to a wider public, working with musicians such as Paloma Faith. His weekly show explores all types of classical and classically inspired music, from Baroque to neo-classical along with classical works infused with folk, jazz, soul and electronic elements.

He describes his work as 'borderless' but having a 'classical signature in its DNA'.[10] His version of 'The Last Post' adds a dignified and thoughtful piano element to the familiar bugle call.

ST ANDREW'S DAY

'A Mhaighdean Bhan Uasal' from *Brave*
2012
Patrick Doyle (1953-)

The 2012 animated Pixar film *Brave* tells the story of Merida, a medieval Scottish princess in the Highlands who very much has a mind of her own, but after a meeting with a witch she accidentally turns her mother into a bear and has to save the kingdom from war. Not only does the film have a large Scottish cast, including Kelly Macdonald as Merida, Billy Connolly as her father King Fergus, and Robbie Coltrane as a combative clan leader, it also features an original song in traditional Scottish Gaelic 'A Mhaighdean Bhan Uasal'.

It was written by Scottish composer Patrick Doyle with words by his son Patrick Neil Doyle as a lullaby, sung as a duet by a young Merida (Peigi Barker) with her mother, Queen Elinor (Emma Thompson). It's also a song about belonging ('Our young Lady, grow and see/Your land, your own faithful land') and honour. The song's title translates into English as 'Noble Maiden Fair'. Thompson does well as a non-speaker, though is not quite as accurate as Barker who had already studied the language and had some experience of singing at traditional Gaelic cultural festivals ('fèis').

Doyle's score for the film is filled with plenty of traditional instruments, including the bodhran drum and bagpipes, as well as Scottish dances such as strathspeys. 'I employed many classic Scottish dance rhythms which not only serve the action but keep it authentic,' said Doyle, who has provided the music for *Sense and Sensibility* (1995),

Gosford Park (2001), *Calendar Girls* (2003) and *Harry Potter and the Goblet of Fire* (2005) as well as more than a dozen films with Kenneth Branagh. For 'A Mhaighdean Bhan Uasal', the harp and solo fiddle provide a tender accompaniment to the touching lullaby. The tune returns later in the film in 'We've Both Changed' at a key point when Merida bids to rescue her mother.

An additional authentic musical element was provided by the popular singer Julie Fowlis, an island native of North Uist in the Outer Hebrides, who sings two original songs on the soundtrack. Until this point Fowlis had only performed and recorded professionally in Gaelic, so the move to English was quite a momentous one for her. However, she did also perform in Gaelic in one of the trailers, singing a truncated version of 'Tha Mo Ghaol Air Aird a' Chuain' (My Love is on the High Seas), a song about a woman's love for a sailor, which is entirely unconnected to the plot of the film. It appears on her album *Mar a tha mo chridhe* (As My Heart Is).

CHRISTMAS

'Troika' from *Lieutenant Kijé*
1934
Sergei Prokofiev (1891–1953)

Perhaps the sound most associated with Christmas in the northern hemisphere is sleigh bells and this jaunty ice-cold journey in a Russian sleigh is about as festive as you can get in three minutes.

Sergei Prokofiev had a knack for telling stories through his music (see pages 7 and 140) and the commission to write the soundtrack to the 1934 Russian film *Lieutenant Kijé* (*Poruchik Kizhe* in Russian, and available in glorious black and white on YouTube) was a perfect opportunity for his first outing in the genre. At first the composer was reluctant to accept but then decided the opportunity of writing music that would be heard by a mass audience was too hard to turn down.

The satirical story about the lengths people go to in order to please their bosses is set in 18th-century Russia at the time of Tsar Paul I. A clerk accidentally adds a non-existent soldier – Kijé – to the army ranks and rather than admit the mistake in front of the Tsar, blames the fictitious fighter for an incident in the palace. The Tsar orders him to be sent to Siberia, then pardons him and Kijé begins an incredibly successful military career, even marrying a princess. Eventually the courtiers are forced to kill him off and blame him for stealing from the Tsar, whereupon he is demoted back to the ranks.

The 'Troika' section comes after the wedding and before the mythical Kijé's 'death'. The music is based on an old Hussar cavalry song and it's a lively dash through the snow (a troika is an old-fashioned

Russian sleigh pulled by horses) with plenty to do for the percussion section of the orchestra, especially the sleigh bells. Alongside, the violins play Kijé's musical motif pizzicato fashion, plucking their strings. It is often played as a stand-alone piece and has been recycled in a jazzy version called 'Midnight Sleighride' as well as the central element in 'I Believe in Father Christmas' by Greg Lake in 1975 who slowed the pace of the troika considerably.

Prokofiev actually spent more time reworking the film score into a 20-minute orchestral suite divided into five movements than he did writing the original soundtrack. His aim was to charm audiences who were new to concert music. 'Above all, it must be melodious,' he said. 'Moreover the melody must be simple and comprehensible without being repetitive or trivial.'[1] As with many of his other works, the very hummable tunes hide some creative touches, such as a double bass playing as high as a violin, and unusual use of the tenor saxophone in an orchestral composition.

'Somewhere in My Memory'
from *Home Alone*
1990
John Williams (1932-)

American composer John Williams has an incredible gift for writing music that seems a natural fit for films, whether they're set in a school for wizards or a galaxy far, far away. For the 1990 film *Home Alone*, he put together something which, like all great soundtracks, helps to move the story along, illuminates it, but draws back when necessary to allow the action to speak for itself. In fact it's been suggested that the film's astonishing success is in some ways due to its music, which was nominated for an Academy Award.

In the film, as the McCallister family leave their Chicago home in a rush for a Christmas holiday in Paris, they accidentally leave the youngest member of the family, Kevin, home alone. He has fun, cleverly foils the plans of a couple of inept burglars and nobody's Christmas ends up being spoiled.

Williams was in fact director Chris Columbus's second choice for providing the film score and he asked him to come up with something reminiscent of the colourful signature sound of Prokofiev (see pages 7, 91 and 140). The soundtrack he delivered uses traditional Christmas songs and carols – look out for 'O Holy Night', 'Carol of the Bells', 'We Wish You a Merry Christmas', 'White Christmas' and 'Jingle Bells' among many others – but the theme that runs throughout the film is the entirely original 'Somewhere in My Memory'. This was written in collaboration with lyricist Leslie Bricusse who had already scored the Albert Finney version of *A Christmas Carol* in 1970 and written showstoppers including 'Feeling Good' and the lyrics for 'Goldfinger'.

'Somewhere in My Memory' is a lovely song that has enjoyed a life outside the movie as one of the few new Christmas songs with genuine longevity. It opens the film with some traditional tinkle from synthetic chimes, celeste and glockenspiel, adds the woodwind and strings, though underneath the Christmas razzamatazz and sleigh bells there are hints of darker undertones of the devilry to come. Then a children's choir sings Bricusse's tear-jerking song about Christmas magic, music and memory with all the family around. As they finish, the whole orchestra takes up the baton until it finally returns to the percussion section. It's not the last time we are presented with the theme as it reprises frequently in numerous scenes as a kind of backbone throughout the film and brings it to a close.

A Spanish version of it – '*Sombras de otros tiempos*' – is also beautifully sung by the Spanish actress and singer Ana Belén in the sequel *Home Alone 2: Lost in New York*.

Overture from *The Muppet Christmas Carol* 1992
Paul Williams (1940-)
and Miles Goodman (1948-1996)

There have been several film versions of Charles Dickens' *A Christmas Carol* but top of many people's lists is the wonderful musical comedy version performed by the Muppets. Ably supported by Michael Caine, it is remarkably faithful to the original story, give or take the usual Muppet tomfoolery. The familiar story of Ebenezer Scrooge's redemption at the hands of various spirits has a particular echo in the soundtrack since the co-composer Paul Williams has also been on a journey from darkness to light.

Williams has a long history of songwriting and composing including 'Rainy Days and Mondays' for The Carpenters, the Academy Award-winning 'Evergreen' for Barbra Streisand's version of *A Star Is Born*, and the Academy Award-nominated 'Rainbow Connection' for Kermit the Frog from the earlier (1979) *Muppet Movie*. But a successful career, including various acting roles, derailed in the 1980s when he became dependent on alcohol and various other substances. As he puts it, he misplaced a decade and by 1989 was enduring psychotic episodes. At this point, Williams realised that he needed help and happily managed to get back on track the following year.

One of his first major jobs once he became clean was *The Muppet Christmas Carol*, co-composed with Miles Goodman. Writing songs about the metamorphosis of the miser turned hero, was what he described as 'my inventory of dealing with where I am in my own life.'[12] Indeed, the film's director Brian Henson commented that Williams empathised very strongly with Scrooge's salvation story, while Oscar Castro-Neves, who orchestrated the music for the film, described him as like a new person to work with.

The upbeat overture that opens the movie plays over the opening titles as the camera swoops around a snowy Victorian London. It starts with a festive trumpet solo and sleigh bells which are joined by the very Muppet combination of a comically huge tuba and a tiny piccolo flute, a brass ensemble and then a glockenspiel to add some yuletide glitter. There are snippets of 'Good King Wenceslas' and 'Hark The Herald Angels Sing' as well as hints of the songs arriving later in the film before the camera glides past a busy street scene and settles on the film's narrator, The Great Gonzo as Dickens . . .

O Magnum Mysterium
1994
Morten Lauridsen (1943-)

In Morten Lauridsen's moving setting of the advent chant *O Magnum Mysterium*, the most important element in the piece is a single note.

Lauridsen is America's most popular living choral composer and he spent six months perfecting the work. It's often sung at Midnight Mass, but Scala Radio plays it 12 months a year. The Latin text talks of the great mystery (*magnum mysterium*) and wonderful sacrament of the animals who witnessed the newborn Lord lying in a manger.

There have been many settings of the words over the centuries, and Lauridsen's composition is a really tender one, with intense layers of floating voices and harmonies gradually building to the birth of Christ. It makes atmospheric use of a technique whereby single syllables are sung across a series of different notes to emphasise them.

Lauridsen felt his major problem was how to portray Mary adequately, and her pride at her son's birth as well as her sadness at his death. As he puts it 'a deeply felt religious statement, at once uncomplicated and unadorned yet powerful and transformative in its effect upon the listener'.[13] He found particular inspiration in an apparently simple painting by the 17th-century Spanish artist Francisco de Zurbarán entitled *Still Life With Lemons, Oranges and A Rose* (1633). This represents Mary using direct yet understated iconography.

In the end, Lauridsen depicted Mary's sorrow by using a single note to highlight the word Virgo (virgin), which stands out quite hauntingly. Lauridsen calls it the most important note in the piece, 'as if a sonic light has suddenly been focused upon it'.[13]

'Andante quasi lento' from *Carol Symphony*
1927
Victor Hely-Hutchinson (1901-1947)

One of the annual traditions that sadly went by the wayside in the pandemic lockdown of 2020 was the carol concert, that time of the year when almost everybody stretches their vocal chords and choirs up and down the country are at their busiest. One of the finest blends of yuletide favourites is *Carol Symphony* by Victor Hely-Hutchinson, the unfortunately now largely forgotten British composer, music critic and teacher. Fittingly, Victor Hely-Hutchinson was born on Boxing Day, in Cape Town, South Africa. He was a musical child prodigy before moving into academia and then broadcasting.

There are four sections to his symphony, each focusing on variations around a different carol but with musical hints of others. It starts with 'O Come All Ye Faithful', which is followed by 'God Rest Ye Merry Gentlemen', and finishes with 'Here We Come A Wassailing'.

Sandwiched in the middle is a much slower, more thoughtful section with 'The Coventry Carol' and 'The First Nowell'. Its 'Andante quasi lento' segment with a slightly mysterious introductory harp theme is the nostalgic highlight for many listeners since it was used as the theme tune to a 1943 radio production of John Masefield's classic Christmas children's book, *The Box of Delights*. It then delighted a later generation in 1984 when a new television series reused it to open and close each episode.

'Have Yourself a Merry Little Christmas'
1944
Hugh Martin (1914-2011)
and Ralph Blane (1914-1995)

You think you know a song and then it turns out it has a history you'd never imagined. 'Have Yourself a Merry Little Christmas' is one of those songs – another is 'You're The Top' – where the lyrics have changed quite dramatically over the years.

1943: Part 1

Hugh Martin and Ralph Blane write the song – though Martin claims he actually did all the heavy lifting – for Judy Garland to sing in the 1944 film *Meet Me in St. Louis*. The scene is Christmas Eve 1903, and Judy and her little sister are facing an unwanted family house move from their home in Missouri to New York. To cheer her sister up, Judy sings her a song which starts:

> Have yourself a merry little Christmas.
> It may be your last.
> Next year we may all be living in the past.

If that's not bad enough, it continues:

> No good times like the olden days.
> Happy golden days of yore.
> Faithful friends who were dear to us.
> Will be near to us no more.

and ends:

> From now on, we'll have to muddle through somehow.

It's not much to really look forward to. Garland and her co-star Tom Drake point this out to the songwriters and ask for something frankly a bit less depressing.

1943: Part 2

Although Martin remarks that it is supposed to be a sad scene, he takes the point and comes back with some adjusted lyrics before filming starts:

> Have yourself a merry little Christmas
> Let your heart be light
> Next year all our troubles will be out of sight.

These are agreed to be much better (although in the film, the little sister is still so upset that she rushes outside and in a rage bashes up their snowmen). The film is a great success and the song becomes a big hit for Garland when she releases it in 1944, a particular favourite for US servicemen.

1957

Now it's Frank Sinatra's turn to request something happier. Again, Martin takes his pen to the song and replaces:

From now on, we'll have to muddle through somehow.

with the more festive:

Hang a shining star upon the highest bough.

It's the version with which most people are familiar today and goes on to be recorded by a huge number of major stars from Ella Fitzgerald (a very jaunty approach) to Michael Bublé and Sam Smith. Garland's daughter Lorna Luft sang a virtual duet version with her mother in 1995.

2001

The final makeover by Martin, a devout Seventh-Day Adventist, is huge as it becomes the much more religious 'Have Yourself a Blessed Little Christmas'. It starts:

Have yourself a blessed little Christmas
Christ the King is born
Let your voices ring upon this happy morn.

and continues in similar vein. It's the same tune but with almost entirely different lyrics.

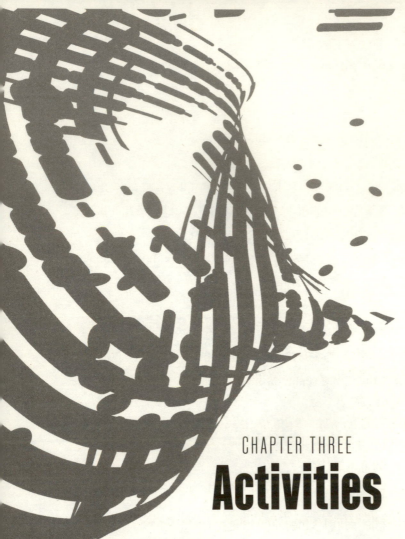

CHAPTER THREE
Activities

BOOKS & READING
'Themes for Narnia' Marisa Robles
'The Scholar' from *Wolf Hall* Debbie Wiseman
'Gypsy Airs' Pablo de Sarasate
'The Tale of the Kalendar Prince' from *Scheherazade*
        Nikolai Rimsky-Korsakov
'Promises to Keep' from *Private Peaceful* Rachel Portman
'Popular Song' from *Façade* Words by Dame Edith Sitwell, music by
        Sir William Walton

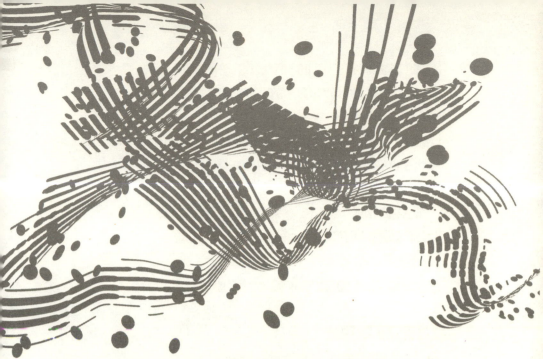

'Pelagia's Song' from *Captain Corelli's Mandolin* Stephen Warbeck
Overture from *Candide* Leonard Bernstein
Overture from *A Midsummer Night's Dream* Felix Mendelssohn
'Once Upon A Time/Storybook Love' from *The Princess Bride*
    Mark Knopfler and Willy DeVille
Symphony No. 9 Ludwig van Beethoven
Main theme from *The Private Life of Sherlock Holmes* Miklós Rózsa
Main theme from *His Dark Materials* Lorne Balfe
'The Godfather Waltz' Nino Rota
'Chapters' from *The Wife* Jocelyn Pook
'Absalon Fili Mi' Josquin des Prez

FOOD & DRINK
'Champagne aria' from *Don Giovanni* Wolfgang Amadeus Mozart
'Taste of Chocolate' from *Chocolat* Rachel Portman
'Quando m'en vo' ('Musetta's Waltz') from *La Bohème* Giacomo Puccini

'**March Past of the Kitchen Utensils**' Ralph Vaughan Williams

'**March**' from *The Love for Three Oranges* Sergei Prokofiev

'**Kitchen Stories**' Dreamers' Circus

'**Prelude**' from *The Victorian Kitchen Garden Suite* Paul Reade

'**Food Glorious Food**' from *Oliver!* Lionel Bart

'**Libiamo ne' lieti calici**' ('The Drinking Song') from *La Traviata*
    Giuseppe Verdi

'**Dance of the Sugar Plum Fairy**' Pyotr Tchaikovsky

'**The Trout**' Franz Schubert

'**Le Festin**' from *Ratatouille* Michael Giacchino

EXPLORING NATURE

'**The Lark Ascending**' Ralph Vaughan Williams

'**The Cuckoo and the Nightingale**' George Frideric Handel

'**The Banks of Green Willow**' George Butterworth

'**Requiem Aeternam**' Rachel Fuller

'**On Hearing the First Cuckoo in Spring**' Frederick Delius

'**Listen to the Grass Grow**' Catrin Finch

'**I Talk to the Wind**' Music by Ian McDonald, words by Peter Sinfield,
    performed by King Crimson

'**The Goldfinch**' Antonio Vivaldi

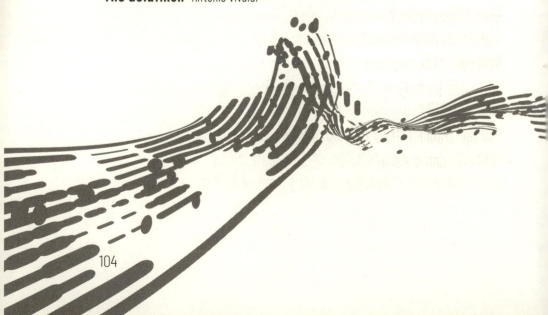

104

Concierto de Aranjuez Joaquín Rodrigo
Main theme from *Avatar* James Horner, performed by The Piano Guys
'Arrival of the Birds' from *The Crimson Wing: The Mystery of the Flamingos* Written by Jason Swinscoe, performed by
The Cinematic Orchestra
Frozen Planet George Fenton

TRANSPORT & TRAVEL

Main theme from *The Simpsons* Danny Elfman
'Short Ride in a Fast Machine' John Adams
'Pleasure Train Polka' Johann Strauss II
Piano Concerto No. 2 Sergei Rachmaninov
Overture from *North by Northwest* Bernard Herrmann
Main theme from *Inspector Morse* Barrington Pheloung
'Lowlands Away' from *Assassin's Creed IV* Traditional/ Brian Tyler
Overture: 'The Hebrides' ('Fingal's Cave') Felix Mendelssohn
Suite one from *Harry Potter and the Cursed Child* Imogen Heap
'Waltz' from *Genevieve* Larry Adler
'Flying' from *E.T. the Extra-Terrestrial* John Williams
'An American in Paris' George Gershwin

BOOKS & READING

'Themes for Narnia'
1981
Marisa Robles (1937-)

The Chronicles of Narnia books for children by C S Lewis have been adapted for stage, film, television, radio and audiobook. One of the best readings is by the English actor Sir Michael Hordern who recorded an abridged version in 1981. Very enjoyable in itself, it benefited from background musical settings by the Spanish harpist Marisa Robles.

So popular was Robles' music that it was made available in its own right as *The Narnia Suite*. 'Themes for Narnia; The Magician; Polly; Digory' is a suitably atmospheric opening track, introducing us to the harp ensemble led by Robles and featuring her then husband, flautist Christopher Hyde-Smith who also plays the piccolo here.

It's all a world away from the more expansive sound created by Harry Gregson-Williams for the 2005 film *The Lion, The Witch and The Wardrobe*. Its sparse twinkling is enigmatic rather than playful to match the magical entry into the land of legendary animals and talking creatures, and the ongoing battle between good and evil.

'The Scholar' from *Wolf Hall*
2015
Debbie Wiseman (1963–)

There is an ongoing and unresolvable argument in music circles about what is meant by attempting to perform music from previous centuries in an 'authentic' way. This means that composing for a period drama is always likely to cause some controversy. For the television adaption of *Wolf Hall*, Hilary Mantel's multi-award-winning fictionalised chronicles of the Tudor statesman Thomas Cromwell, English composer Debbie Wiseman decided to go for a blend of the old and the new.

Wiseman is an experienced hand at writing film scores, often with literary connections, including the 1997 biopic *Wilde* starring Stephen Fry as Oscar and *To Olivia* (2021) about the author Roald Dahl. She is also much in demand for television, everything from the theme to journalist Andrew Marr's political show to *Dickensian* (2015), and she also lectures on the art of composing for the screen, so Wiseman definitely practises what she preaches.

For *Wolf Hall*, there are one or two Tudor pieces in the score that date from the period, but the majority of the music television viewers hear was written by Wiseman. It's not a pastiche, but it does clearly recreate a period atmosphere that somehow also manages to feel contemporary, a deliberate reflection of Mantel's approach in the novels; the music wouldn't feel out of place in a series about modern politicians. It's elegantly captivating.

The score mostly uses instruments that were available in the period. In 'The Scholar' we hear a trio of solos from the recorder (which often indicates the presence of Cromwell, at its most austere in 'Monstrous Servant'), the harpsichord and the vielle, a larger and more oval version of the violin. Elsewhere we are also treated to the theorbo, a cousin of the lute but with a much longer neck, as well as the gorgeous strings of chamber music specialists the Locrian Ensemble.

Wiseman wrote some of the music before shooting began and it was used by director Peter Kosminsky to set the pace of certain scenes. Among them was Cromwell's main theme, 'Wolf Hall/Entirely Beloved', a piece for strings and some of those period instruments that sums up the statesman's unstoppable, machine-like energy as well as his darker side.

If you enjoy Wiseman's work on *Wolf Hall*, you might also like the 15th- and 16th-century dances and songs which also appeared in the television series, played on period instruments, on a second soundtrack album *Wolf Hall: Tudor Music*. They were collected and arranged by Claire van Kampen, founding Director of Music at Shakespeare's Globe Theatre, and wife of Mark Rylance, the actor who played Cromwell in the series.

'Gypsy Airs'
1878
Pablo de Sarasate (1844–1908)

What do you do when you're in the middle of trying to solve a perplexing, maybe even criminal, puzzle? If you're Sherlock Holmes and Dr Watson, naturally you head off to a music concert.

In the 1891 Arthur Conan Doyle short story 'The Red-Headed League', a man with the appropriate coloured hair asks the famous detective if he can sort out a mystery related to some strange work he has recently been paid to do. To help him think things through ('It is quite a three-pipe problem'), Holmes suggests to Watson that they head to St James's Hall, a large concert hall that stood on London's Regent Street and Piccadilly until it was demolished in 1905.

Holmes is attracted in particular to the concert since it is being given by the accomplished Spanish violinist Pablo de Sarasate. 'I observe that there is a good deal of German music on the programme, which is rather more to my taste than Italian or French. It is introspective, and I want to introspect.' Watson watches Holmes working out the solution throughout the concert.

Sarasate was not only a celebrated performer of the day, he was also a composer and, like many of his peers, intrigued by traditional and folk music of his native Spain and other parts of Europe. His most famous piece is 'Zigeunerweisen', or in English 'Gypsy Airs', for violin and orchestra, a dramatic work with romantic slower sections and a lively finale of which no doubt Holmes would have approved. The piece was inspired by Romani music Sarasate enjoyed on a visit to Budapest in the late 1870s.

Actually, this was not Romani but simply Hungarian folk music that Sarasate miscategorised. Indeed, one of the four sections in the eight-minute piece was in fact a melody written by the Hungarian composer Elemér Szentirmay who wrote Sarasate a polite but firm letter pointing this out and equally politely requesting his name should appear on the official sheet music.

There have been numerous recordings of 'Gypsy Airs' over the last century, including Sarasate's own in 1904, which is still available. It also features in Pixar's 2005 short about duelling buskers, *One Man Band*.

'Tale of the Kalendar Prince' from *Scheherazade*
1888
Nikolai Rimsky-Korsakov (1844-1908)

Here is a truly romantic swirling piece to go with one of the finest stories about story-telling. Russian composer Nikolai Rimsky-Korsakov's *Scheherazade* suite is based on *The Arabian Nights/One Thousand and One Nights* tales. The music is as colourful and vibrant as the tales the lovely Scheherazade tells every night to avoid having her head cut off the following morning by the wilfully misogynous Sultan.

Rimsky-Korsakov wrestled with the naming of the various sections of the work he wrote in 1888. Initially he gave them titles such as 'The Sea and Sinbad's Ship', 'The Ship Breaks Against a Cliff Surmounted by a Bronze Horseman', and 'Festival at Baghdad'. But he was keen not to make these separate unconnected episodes correspond closely to well-known voyages of Sinbad and eventually removed them all. He commented in his memoirs that he was simply going for a general 'Oriental' effect telling a story of wonderful fairy tales.

'The Tale of the Kalendar Prince', the second 'story' of the piece, is particularly evocative. It begins with a beautiful violin solo with fluttering harp accompaniment, Scheherazade's own musical signature indicating her narration, and a contrast to the Sultan, represented by sterner brass instruments (although the composer denied that there was any link between musical motifs and characters). Listen out too for the march section played on bassoon. Kalendar here does not refer to the passing of days, but to the kind of highly regarded mystic soothsayer, a beggar who was a familiar wandering figure in the medieval Islamic world. Various Kalendars are mentioned in the original Arabian Nights stories but it's not clear which one this piece focuses on.

Scheherazade has also been adapted as a ballet and its debut production in 1910 by the famed Ballets Russes starring a gold-painted Vaslav Nijinsky was remarkable for its sensationally erotic choreography and lush costumes and scenery. The very upright former naval officer Rimsky-Korsakov died two years before it premiered and almost certainly would not have approved, especially of the orgy scene.

'Promises to Keep' from *Private Peaceful*
2012
Rachel Portman (1960-)

English composer Rachel Portman is one of the leading composers of modern film soundtracks with dozens under her belt including *One Day*, *Never Let Me Go* and *The Duchess*, a score which has recently been a part of the A-level music syllabus. Her work for the 1996 version of *Emma* starring Gwyneth Paltrow won her an Academy Award, making her the first female composer to scoop the award. She was also nominated for an Academy Award for *The Cider House Rules* and *Chocolat* (see page 135).

Her score for the 2012 film version of Michael Morpurgo's novel *Private Peaceful* is one of her most heart-wrenching. The story follows the experiences of two brothers in love and war. At its most lyrical is 'Promises to Keep' a reference to one of the brothers, Tommo, who tells himself he must survive the harrowing events of the battlefield and return home. Interweaving violins suggest the entwined lives and the sadness to come as they dance around each other. Wistfully happy too is 'No Tomorrow Could Ever Be As Good As Today', the musing of Molly, the object of both the young men's hearts.

However, Portman also underlines the grim reality of the brothers' experiences of the First World War in a series of brooding sections. 'Sentry Duty' is among these, offering not a blockbuster threat of menace, but a far more tangible one.

'Popular Song' from *Façade*
1923
Words by Dame Edith Sitwell (1887-1964), music by Sir William Walton (1902-1983)

Opening night, 12 June 1923, the Aelion Hall, London. The great and the good of the capital's arts world including writers Evelyn Waugh and Noel Coward were present to witness the first public performance of Edith Sitwell's poetry collection *Façade* set to music by the then largely unknown composer Sir William Walton.

They were greeted with a stage featuring only a static curtain decorated by painter John Piper as a kind of theatrical backdrop. There was a Gothic house, a lake, a garden and a mask with a large hole where the mouth should have been. Through this, Sitwell declaimed her poems using a decorated megaphone. Alongside her, and also unseen, Walton and half a dozen musicians accompanied the verses. Sitwell described the whole thing as an 'Entertainment', though many among the audience on that first night were just rather bemused.

A century later, it has been recognised as a spectacular fusion of experimental words and music. Sitwell's poems were written to be performed rather than read silently, and play with rhythm and sound rather than focusing on traditional forms. There is meaning, but initially they do sound a little like nonsense, especially if recited at speed (for a first listen, a copy of the words is not a bad idea). Sitwell's aim was to create elaborate rhythms and abstract texture as much as to make sense. It's perhaps a stretch to describe it as early rap, but there are some similarities. If this all sounds a bit weird, well, it is, but it's certainly worth giving it a go.

Walton's music is less unconventional but similarly playful and is often performed without the texts it originally accompanied. *The Times* review described him, approvingly, as a 'musical joker'. The witty original score was for the unusual combination of cello, trumpet, percussion, saxophone, clarinet and flute/piccolo, which gives it a colourful 1920s dance band flavour. It's jazz-influenced rather than classic jazz, with lots of musical quotations from well-known songs and operas in the mix. One of the most famous songs is 'Popular Song', a catchy and memorable tune, though the poem will have most listeners Googling the people name-checked at full tilt by Sitwell. When Frederick Ashton turned *Façade* into a ballet in 1931, he choreographed 'Popular Song' as a tap dance performed by two young men in striped blazers and straw boaters.

Façade was Sitwell's finest literary hour, but Walton went on to great, and far more conventional, things in the classical music world including his 'Crown Imperial' march, which has been performed at coronations since 1937.

'Pelagia's Song'
from *Captain Corelli's Mandolin*
2001
Stephen Warbeck (1953-)

While the 2001 film version of Louis de Bernières' 1994 phenomenal bestseller is a Second World War love triangle set in Cephalonia, Greece, it's also a story of music and how it can offer solace at a time of great trouble.

As the title suggests, the mandolin takes centre stage. Nicolas Cage, who plays Corelli, was so keen to get into his role that despite never having played any musical instrument before, he learned the mandolin. He was taught by the film's musical director Paul Englishby who, incidentally, taught Hugh Grant to play the guitar in the film *About A Boy*. When you watch the film, that really is Cage playing, although for the official soundtrack album professional mandolin player Giovanni Parricelli was drafted in.

The actual score for the film was written by Stephen Warbeck who had previously worked with its director, John Madden, on *Shakespeare in Love*, and his film score CV includes many other hits, among them *Billy Elliot*. At its centre is the romantic 'Pelagia's Song' which Corelli writes for his love, Pelagia played by Penélope Cruz. It's a charmingly understated theme based around just four notes, which is typical of the score's simple and relaxed sound. There's nothing glitzy here, though the score does range from an intensity in the battle scenes to a marvellous tango featuring lively accordions. It took Warbeck a year to write and he completed it before filming started, an unusual but not unique approach in the industry. This also gave Cage the chance to get to grips with the mandolin before shooting began.

With added lyrics about love and the key theme of remembrance, 'Pelagia's Song' is also one of two songs performed by classical crossover artist Russell Watson for the film. The other is 'Senza Di Te' and he does them both justice. As an interesting contrast with a tenor star from a century ago, the soundtrack also features the great Italian tenor Enrico Caruso (1873–1921) performing 'Santa Lucia'.

Overture from *Candide*
1956
Leonard Bernstein (1918–1990)

A mid-18th-century satirical novel poking fun at the fashionable philosophies of the day seems an unlikely basis for a hilarious rollercoaster musical show on Broadway two centuries later. And yet Leonard Bernstein's take on *Candide*, the French writer Voltaire's classic story of optimism and coming of age, is a whirlwind operetta in the style of a witty Gilbert and Sullivan production.

The American Bernstein was much in demand as a conductor, but he also loved composing music and wanted to write 'the great American opera'. Strangely, maybe his *Candide* was it, a work that offered plenty of laughs but also addressed the hysteria of the contemporary anti-communist witch hunts.

The show is quite faithful to the original book. It follows the fortunes of the endlessly hopeful *Candide* as the young man ventures out into the world from a sheltered existence in France where he has been taught that he lives in the best of all possible worlds. He is tortured by the Inquisition (a very thinly disguised reference to those witch hunts), survives a major earthquake, is nearly eaten by Incas and visits El Dorado. There are almost impossible coincidences and resurrections along the way. And not all the characters in *Candide* finish the story with the same number of buttocks with which they started it.

This whistlestop tour of the world is reflected in the energetic bustle of the overture. It starts with a horn fanfare bang and then gallops off with an oom-pah-pah as it previews the main themes to come, the catchy 'The Best Of All Possible Worlds', the witty 'Oh Happy

We' and the grimmer 'Glitter and Be Gay'. There's an especially sweet love motif in the central section and solos for bassoon, piccolo and clarinet before it leaps away at speed again at the end. With plenty of vibrant brass and percussion to give it a real whoomph, it's rhythmic and dynamic and the perfect curtain-raiser to the fun ahead. Jack Pepper, host of Scala Radio's 'Culture Bunker' and a huge fan of Leonard Bernstein, has referred to the composer as 'a storyteller with sound', and describes this as a perfect Overture, 'a call to attention at the start of a show!'

Today, the organised chaos of the overture is extremely popular in concert halls but the show itself had a stormy history. It opened in 1956 and was received quite poorly before numerous major rewrites of the music and book – including additions by American humorist Dorothy Parker and composer Stephen Sondheim – established it as a firm favourite.

Overture from *A Midsummer Night's Dream* 1826
Felix Mendelssohn (1809-1847)

It starts with four faintly mysterious chords. It could barely be any simpler, and yet the spell immediately transports us to a forest outside Athens for William Shakespeare's magical comedy of love and identity, *A Midsummer Night's Dream*.

As a boy, German composer Felix Mendelssohn found this to be one of his favourite plays (though you can't please everybody: London diarist Samuel Pepys wrote in 1662 that it was 'the most insipid ridiculous play that ever I saw in my life'2). Mendelssohn was a child musical genius to rival Mozart and he wrote the overture when he was a teenager.

Performed for the first time in 1827, it's a perfect summary of the action to come. After those first four cryptic chords from the woodwind, which are said to be inspired by the composer listening to wind blowing in the trees, we're into the forest, surrounded by scampering fairies. They are disturbed by the arrival of the Duke of Athens and his hunting horn, the romantic couples, then the weaver Bottom's metamorphosis into a braying donkey. Violins depict the animal's 'hee-haw' now, but originally Mendelssohn used an ophicleide, a forerunner of the tuba. Finally, those four chords return and drift away. The whole thing fizzes along over hill, over dale, and it's all very entertaining.

Mendelssohn returned to the play 15 years later to write additional music to go with a theatre production including his famous 'Wedding March'. Of the many recordings of this and the overture, the one conducted by Seiji Ozawa for Deutsche Grammophon in 1994 (which includes the actor Dame Judi Dench reciting parts of the play) is one of the finest. It serves as a reminder that Mendelssohn's overture was music written to be played between scenes at the theatre to add atmosphere, not wholly unlike our film scores and film adaptions: Max Reinhardt's in 1935 and Woody Allen's in 1982 have both made good use of it.

'Once Upon A Time/Storybook Love' from *The Princess Bride*
1987
Mark Knopfler (1949-)
and Willy DeVille (1950-2009)

The 1987 film *The Princess Bride* is based on the fairy-tale book of the same name by William Goldman (who also wrote the screenplay), so it definitely required a fairy-tale soundtrack. Yet like the book it's also much more peculiar than a normal fairy tale so it would be inconceivable to make it too schmaltzy or swashbuckling. Happily, nobody had to get used to disappointment and Mark Knopfler – on a break from duties with Dire Straits who were at the peak of their popularity – provided a simple if slightly quirky score that fits like a hand in a glove.

The opening track is American singer-songwriter Willy DeVille's 'Once Upon A Time/Storybook Love', arranged by Knopfler, introducing the sweet acoustic guitar with drifting synthesiser sounds that form the film's romantic core theme. It's warm and friendly and won Willy DeVille and Knopfler a nomination for Best Original Song at the 1988 Academy Awards. Also memorable is the amusingly clip-cloppy 'The Friends' Song'. It's not all happily ever after though. Elsewhere, Knopfler builds up some mild peril with 'Cliffs of Insanity' and menace with 'The Fireswamp'.

It could all have been quite a different sound as director Rob Reiner initially asked Paul McCartney to come up with incidental music for the much loved film. McCartney sent him 'Once Upon a Long Ago' (which he envisaged as a duet for himself and Freddie Mercury) and 'Beautiful Night', but Reiner wasn't keen and turned to Knopfler. McCartney has since recorded both songs so it's possible to listen to what could have been.

Symphony No. 9
1824
Ludwig van Beethoven (1770-1827)

As a young man, novelist Anthony Burgess wanted to become a composer, and even in later life said he preferred to be known as a musician who wrote novels rather than a novelist who dabbled in music. Burgess wrote a symphony and often included musical elements in his books, especially *Napoleon Symphony* which was modelled on Beethoven's 'Eroica' Symphony. The composer's choral Symphony No. 9 was centre-stage in Burgess's disturbingly dystopian novel *A Clockwork Orange*. This was even more apparent when it was filmed by Stanley Kubrick in 1971.

Rather than choose pop music – which Burgess hated, calling it 'twanging nonsense'[3] – as the expected listening choice of Alex the book's degenerate lead character, the author chose Beethoven's Symphony No. 9, generally regarded as the composer's masterpiece. It was a bold selection, Burgess inferring not only that the violent Alex was quite sophisticated, but also that Beethoven's music was as enticing and tempestuous as anything available in the pop charts. The inference was that the only meaning in a piece of music is what we decide to see in it.

The Ninth is a remarkable work, both stirring and lyrical, usually interpreted as a call for the end of political repression and an optimistic cry for all sectors of society to come together in one humanitarian whole. For its premiere in 1824, it required the biggest orchestra Beethoven had ever put together for his symphonies and, unusually, included a technically very demanding sung section, the 'Ode to Joy', in the fourth and final movement. Although it's been adopted by racist regimes, it's often also sung at moments of genuine celebration around the world and was later named as the 'Anthem of Europe' by the European Union. In the film, composer Wendy Carlos adapted the tune for 'vocoder', a voice synthesiser.

Music is absolutely central to the sociopathic Alex's life and Beethoven's symphonies are his musical motif throughout the film from the notes that sound when he rings a doorbell to his almost drug-like ecstasy on hearing the Ninth. Later in the film, when it is taken away from him, he is distraught. Certainly, once you've seen *A Clockwork Orange*, you'll never listen to Beethoven in the same way again.

Main theme from *The Private Life of Sherlock Holmes*
1970
Miklós Rózsa (1907-1995)

Billy Wilder was one of the finest film directors of the 20th century and *The Private Life of Sherlock Holmes* was set to be one of his final masterpieces. Starring Robert Stephens as the consulting detective and Christopher Lee as his brother Mycroft, it's a slightly tongue-in-cheek homage to the great man which takes in ballet, the Loch Ness monster, a beautiful woman on the hunt for her missing husband, and Queen Victoria.

However, once it was finished studio bosses baulked at the projected three-hour running time and without Wilder's agreement it was hacked right back by more than an hour. It's still a wonderful film and partly inspired the writers of the modern *Sherlock* version with Benedict Cumberbatch, though it does feel like a project that wasn't fully realised.

Fortunately, one thing that didn't get the chop was the marvellous soundtrack by Hungarian composer Miklós Rózsa.

Music was part of the 1970 film from the very beginning. Wilder planned the script as a kind of four movement symphony and wrote the screenplay while listening to Rózsa's 1953 violin concerto in the background on repeat. The pair had already worked together on several films including the 1945 film noir *The Lost Weekend*. When Wilder approached the composer about providing a soundtrack, Rózsa – as big a fan as Wilder of the fictional investigator - was delighted and used his concerto as the kernel around which the rest of the score was formed.

At its heart is the elegant love theme for solo violin, which Rózsa had originally written for the violin maestro Jascha Heifetz, and which is also an appropriate nod to Holmes's own ability on the instrument. It anticipates a terrible sadness ahead (although the first hour of the film is actually remarkably perky). The theme also contains passages of stately joie de vivre and dramatic mystery and it reappears at important points in the action, especially in the romantic but somewhat uneasy 'Gabrielle'. The soundtrack recording is particularly valuable for fans of the film since it includes 20 minutes of additional music, which disappeared when the film was cut.

After a long career scoring films in Hollywood including *The Thief of Bagdad* and *Ben-Hur*, this was one of Rózsa's last major commissions. His final work was for Steve Martin's black-and-white *Dead Men Don't Wear Plaid*, a 1982 comedy which paid homage to, and included snippets from, the kind of 1940s films on which Rózsa had cut his filmic music teeth.

Main theme from *His Dark Materials* 2019
Lorne Balfe (1976-)

Writing music for a film version of a book that has very devoted followers is a tricky business: there are legions of fans who are very keen indeed not to be disappointed. The first to have a go at scoring Philip Pullman's story of love, religion and parallel universes was French composer Alexandre Desplat. He worked on the big budget 2007 Hollywood version of the first part, *The Golden Compass*. Despite its superb score, the film underperformed at the box office but the television version, which premiered in 2019, was very well received.

Scottish composer Lorne Balfe has acknowledged how testing it is to write a 60-second piece of music to introduce viewers to a new world, something that represents the emotions of the books. Happily, his captivating title theme to the television series of *His Dark Materials* provided the right stuff from the very beginning: this is an epic march for piano and orchestra that fans of the *Westworld* television series music will enjoy. It's appropriately titanic to match the struggles to come on-screen, with an understated vocal backbone as it reaches a crescendo.

Each character has a theme, the heroine Lyra's appropriately mysterious but growing darker as the series progresses, the enigmatic Mrs Coulter's sparklingly sinister. Medieval choral music is the keynote of the distinctly unsettling 'A New Cardinal Rises' and there's a modern folk music feel to 'Scholastic Sanctuary'.

Balfe enjoyed the books and was keen to be a part of the production from the moment the television series was announced. Partly inspired by examples of graphic art he pinned on the wall next to his keyboard, he even submitted some musical suggestions well before he won the commission. For the second series – voted by Scala Radio listeners their favourite television music of 2020 – he revealed that the trauma of the coronavirus pandemic also stimulated his imagination.

'What I wanted people to feel when listening to the music is they don't necessarily know if it's real or not or whether it's in the present or in the past,' Balfe said when the music was unveiled. 'There are no rules and musically, it's constantly evolving.'[4] To provide this enigmatic sound, which Balfe described as Elgar meets Nine Inch Nails, he assembled an eclectic team including the Red Hot Chili Peppers' drummer Chad Smith. It also includes cellist Tina Guo, a key part of *Journey* (see page 36) who makes her mark in the powerful 'Strength of Gyptians', and recorder specialist Richard Harvey whose wooden flute work is memorably melancholic.

Balfe worked under film-score composing legend Hans Zimmer and has provided the music for major releases such as *Mission: Impossible – Fallout* and *Black Widow*, *The Crown* television series, as well as the *Assassin's Creed* and *Call of Duty* video game series.

'The Godfather Waltz'
1972
Nino Rota (1911-1979)

From the opening bars of *The Godfather*, it's clear that we're not in screwball comedy territory. The trumpet's first melancholy solo in 'The Godfather Waltz' – which we hear over the ominously black opening titles before any of the action starts – indicates that this is a story about the man at the top, sometimes a chillingly lonely place to be. It pierces the darkness, but it doesn't provide any reassurance.

Italian composer Nino Rota provided the score for the film based on the 1969 book of the same name by Mario Puzo about the Italian-American mafia in the US. Rota was incredibly productive, writing a dozen operas and ballets, as well as choral works, music for theatre productions and some 150 film soundtracks. For *The Godfather* he also reused some of his music from his earlier film *Fortunella* (1958) for the equally famous 'Love Theme', which got him into hot water with the Academy Award nominations committee.

Rota understandably opted for an Italian feel to the music and 'The Godfather Waltz' is a perfect example of the deliberately folky flavour he gave it. After the trumpet finishes its haunting solo, the accordion and mandolin come in, emphasising that sense of tradition with the mafia family's homeland in Sicily. By the end of the first couple of minutes, we have a strong feeling of nostalgia and a sense of the human tragedy about to unfold as the melody repeats and repeats. It returns plaintively later in the film associated with the eponymous Godfather Vito Corleone (and at the end as power is transferred to his heir Michael) and in the sequel, sometimes with the trumpet's main role replaced by another instrument, most memorably the oboe.

Rota's mafia waltz also crops up in the novelist Kazuo Ishiguro's interlocking short-story collection from 2009 *Nocturnes*. Here its international popularity is apparent as one of the tunes that busking musicians play to bank on making money in tourist hotspots like Venice. One character remarks that in a single afternoon the previous summer he played it nine times after lunch.

'Chapters' from *The Wife*
2017
Jocelyn Pook (1960-)

Joseph (Jonathan Pryce) and Joan Castleman (Glenn Close) have had a long and successful marriage, so successful that novelist Joseph is about to be awarded the Nobel prize in literature. But behind closed doors, *The Wife* (2017) gradually reveals that there are more than cracks in their relationship.

The film's soundtrack by English composer Jocelyn Pook is ubiquitously dramatic and resolutely fails to offer much optimism as things fall apart. There's a bittersweet current to the reflective wheeling violins of 'Chapters', a complex sensation that runs through the rest of the score. There's no threat, but plenty of regret as the music explores a life spent in the shadows – Pook has talked about her music offering 'another voice' in film. It's pared down and understated rather than minimalist but Pook has acknowledged the influence of Philip Glass, Michael Nyman and Arvo Pärt, and the shape of their soundscapes is evident here.

Pook was catapulted to fame by her first feature film score for Stanley Kubrick's *Eyes Wide Shut*, but she has a long and varied history in the music business. As well as her scores for film, theatre and television, she's worked with Massive Attack, Nick Cave and Paul Weller, and was a core member of The Communards, playing the viola. More recently she has set to music excerpts of speeches by environmentalist Greta Thunberg in 'You Need To Listen To Us' featuring the National Youth Choir of Great Britain.

'Absalon Fili Mi'
c. 1500
Josquin des Prez (c.1450-1521)

It's possible to produce a really good mix tape of the music mentioned in many novels. Among them is *The Time of our Singing* (2003) by American physicist, musician and writer Richard Powers in which he namechecks a huge range of composers and works from Renaissance lutenist John Dowland to The Beatles. It's the story of a musical family spanning much of the 20th century with the issue of race at its core. The key event is the enormous and defiantly antiracist open-air concert given in 1939 in Washington DC on the steps of the Lincoln Memorial by black singer Marian Anderson. The novel is also a meditation on the power of playing and listening to music.

Parents David and Delia have three children and much of their family time revolves around music. One game they all play together is called 'Crazed Quotations' in which they improvise a kind of musical conversation competition by singing snatches of different musical forms to each other. During one of these sessions, the oldest child, Jonah, sings a perfect version of 'Absalon Fili Mi' by French composer Josquin des Prez, one of the leading composers of the Renaissance.

'Absalon Fili Mi' is an incredibly tricky song for a nine-year old and his choice quite rightly amazes his parents. It is a lament by King David about the death of his son Absalom as recounted in the book of Samuel in the Bible. It's probably Josquin's best-known piece, written for four voices as a sacred motet. While the text about the loss of a child is terribly sad, the music is not so melancholic, and the harmonies are perfect.

FOOD & DRINK

'Champagne aria' from *Don Giovanni*
1787
Wolfgang Amadeus Mozart (1756-1791)

As opera arias go, this is fast and furious, requiring well under two minutes to perform. But what a thrilling, tongue-twisting performance.

It comes from the marvellous *Don Giovanni*, written in 1787 when Wolfgang Amadeus Mozart was at the height of his genius. Based on the legendary activity of the infamous seducer Don Juan, the plot essentially follows the exploits of the flashy young nobleman Don Giovanni as he spends his time unapologetically duelling, killing, eating and womanising. This is the aria – officially known as *'Fin ch'han dal vino'* – which perhaps best sums up his very un-PC approach to life. It takes place towards the end of Act I. Don Giovanni is with his servant Leporello and instructing him how to make preparations for a large party.

Let's have plenty of wine until we're sloshed, he tells him. Nip out to the town square and invite plenty of women because I'm in the mood for some wild dancing and lovemaking. By tomorrow morning, he boasts, my list of conquests will have ten more names on it.

It's all sung at breakneck speed to accompany the energetic way the young rake leads his life, with other people valued only so far as they can satisfy his desires.

There's no doubt that the Don is a terrible man, selfish and thoughtless, but it's a hugely catchy aria and there is also something quite thrilling about watching him relish his lifestyle so thoroughly. However, some critics have detected an element of slight desperation in the song, that Don Giovanni is actually rather bored of life. Which – slight spoiler alert – is about to be derailed in a most supernatural way at the end of Act II when he comes up against an old enemy . . .

The opera plays a key part in the 1984 film *Amadeus*, based on the play by Peter Schaffer, and was also updated for a 1990 movie version, directed by American theatre director Peter Sellars and set in Harlem. For this, the seediness of the anti-hero was dialled up to 10, Don Giovanni smashing multiple bottles of champagne as he sings, then finishing by shooting up heroin. In fact, although it's called the 'Champagne aria', Don Giovanni never mentions the drink once and it's a bit of a mystery how it got its name.

'Taste of Chocolate' from *Chocolat*
2000
Rachel Portman (1960-)

English composer Rachel Portman was classically trained in music at the University of Oxford, but her preference was always for film rather than classical composition. One of her earliest works, as an undergraduate, was for a student film starring her contemporary Hugh Grant and since then she has written extensively for film, television and theatre, including a musical version of Laura Ingalls Wilder's book *The Little House on the Prairie*.

The 2000 film *Chocolat* is based on the novel of the same name by English author Joanne Harris, which places food, especially chocolate in its many forms, front and centre. At the start of Lent, the mysterious Vianne Rocher arrives in a small rural French village to open a chocolaterie in the old bakery. Her presence and her produce have a surprising effect on the locals' traditional lifestyles. Portman was not the first choice to score the comedy-drama film. Director Lasse Hallström was not pleased with the first-choice composer so turned to Portman who had less than a month to come up with a replacement. This did not stop her earning an Academy Award nomination for her work on the film.

In keeping with the content of the film, the music is quite impish and magical with a particular emphasis on woodwind instruments. The 'Taste of Chocolate' track adds a sweepingly dramatic element to proceedings but the overall sound is not a dominatingly bombastic one. 'I'm interested in trying to express emotion and humanity,'[5] Portman said in an interview for Scala Radio, and while she can certainly write wonderfully for full orchestras, she has a knack for summing up a scene or a person without going over the top. Her music feels very personal – it's not possible to really identify a signature 'Portman sound' – and here she avoids falling into the trap of making the soundtrack too sickly sweet. She has described the character of Vianne as having a 'restless exhaustive quality' and this is certainly reflected in the music.

'Quando m'en vo' ('Musetta's Waltz') from *La Bohème*
1896
Giacomo Puccini (1858–1924)

It's Christmas Eve in Paris. Cold and hungry in his garret, painter Marcello sets off to look for food with his friends Colline (a philosopher) and Schaunard (a musician), leaving behind his friend the poet Rodolfo to get on with some writing. Meanwhile, their sickly seamstress neighbour Mimi appears at the door, having lost the key to her dwelling. She and Rodolfo talk, suddenly romance is in the air, and they set off after Marcello . . .

We're in Act II of Giacomo Puccini's 1896 opera *La Bohème* and about to hear one of the most famous soprano arias, *'Quando m'en vo'* or 'Musetta's Waltz'.

The setting is the Café Momus, which existed in real life, the second home of the artistic bohemians of the opera's title. There's plenty of bustle as street vendors shout out to sell their food and gifts, and the group of friends sit and chat about love. Suddenly, Marcello's old flame, Musetta, enters. Although she is with her new elderly sugar daddy, Alcindoro, she immediately starts flirting with Marcello and sings the gorgeous 'Quando m'en vo' ('As I walk' in English) in a bid to get him back.

It's a short but pretty shameless aria. Musetta describes how people stop and stare at her beauty, from head to foot, when she walks alone through the streets. And she admits that seeing their desire makes her happy. She ends by suggesting to Marcello that the memory of their time together is getting him all hot under the collar . . .

It works. Musetta sends Alcindoro away on a pointless errand, she and Marcello are reunited and, for the moment, everybody has a good time, eating and drinking to their hearts' content. Food is one of the major themes of the opera – the characters switch between feast and famine several times.

The aria has been recorded by a host of major opera stars including Anna Moffo, Maria Callas and Dame Kiri Te Kanawa, though one of the most beguiling is by the Russian-Austrian soprano Anna Netrebko. 'Musetta's Waltz' also features in Jonathan Larson's 1994 musical *Rent*, the loose updating of *La Bohème* against the background of the spread of AIDS/HIV. Penny Smith, Scala Radio's resident opera fanatic, recommends *La Bohème* as a great place to start if you're a first-timer, describing it as 'one of the most instantly approachable of Puccini's operas. Access all emotions.'

'March Past of the Kitchen Utensils'
1909
Ralph Vaughan Williams (1872-1958)

The plot of the comedy *The Wasps* by Aristophanes, first performed in 422 BC, focuses on a man who has become obsessed with the law and law courts of ancient Athens, and his children's efforts to help him deal with his fixation. In a bid to calm him down, they encourage him to stage his own trial at home where they have put him under virtual house arrest. They arrange him to judge in a case in which one of his pet dogs has accused the other of stealing some cheese. To add some authenticity to the proceedings, there naturally need to be witnesses, and this is where the contents of the kitchen drawers come in. These witnesses/kitchen utensils include a cheese grater, a bowl, a pestle and mortar and a pot (a 2005 recording adds a wok) that march along to the punctuation of the cymbals.

A version of the comedy was produced in Oxford in 1909, for which English composer Ralph Vaughan Williams wrote his suite of incidental music. It contains five sections and while it's not played or performed much in its entirety, the 'Overture' and the appealing 'March Past of the Kitchen Utensils' are popular stand-alone pieces.

One of the instructions to the percussionist playing the piece is that they must 'shake a bag of broken china'. The story goes that at the premiere, one of the performers lightheartedly asked Vaughan Williams if it should be Wedgwood, knowing that he was a member of the famous Staffordshire pottery family. The composer replied yes, since it was the only china that would make the right sound.

'March' from *The Love for Three Oranges*
1921
Sergei Prokofiev (1891-1953)

While Russian composer Sergei Prokofiev's *Petrushka* (see page 13) has a most unusual plot, his 1921 opera *The Love for Three Oranges* runs it very close. Based on an 18th-century Italian play, it tells of a handsome prince whose father is King of Trifles. A bungling witch accidentally cures him of depression then casts a spell to make him fall in love with three oranges which she tasks him to seek. Various adventures later, he finds them, peels them and – spoiler alert – finds a princess in each, the loveliest of which he marries and all's well that ends well.

Like much of Prokofiev's work, what sounds appealing to 21st-century ears was far more challenging to listeners a century ago. It was deliberately avant-garde, almost pantomime-like in places, Prokofiev's contribution to fight what he saw as too much realism in contemporary theatre. It has no delightful or dramatic arias, and the whole fanciful concept is of a play within a play. Music critics were harsh – 'Russian jazz with Bolshevik trimmings' complained one – although audiences took to it more quickly. It is now regularly performed, including a 1998 production for which audiences received scratch 'n' sniff cards for appropriate moments (naturally, among them was the whiff of oranges).

The most famous piece is the stirring but slightly surreal 'March' which is used a number of times to indicate the rather odd atmosphere at the royal court. Woody Allen used it for a similar reason to poke fun at Napoleon in his 1975 film *Love and Death* and it was rather bizarrely also used by the American television series *The FBI in Peace and War* as its theme tune in the 1940s and 1950s. It also makes a little guest appearance in the composer's ballet *Cinderella* (see page 7).

'Kitchen Stories'
2018
Dreamers' Circus

Folk music has been enjoying a resurgence in the UK in recent years and has encouraged people to widen their musical horizons beyond its shores. One of the finest European groups to emerge since the millennium is the Scandinavian instrumental trio, Dreamers' Circus, who offer a varied Nordic folk sound that has been a big hit at the annual Celtic Connections festivals.

It's also a marvellously varied sound. The Danish jazz pianist Nikolaj Busk also plays harpsichord and accordion, and his fellow countryman Rune Tonsgaard Sørensen is a highly regarded classical violinist as well as being proficient on the clog fiddle (basically a violin with a clog body), harmonium and vibraphone. Ale Carr from Sweden plays the Nordic cittern (similar to a mandolin), kokle (a plucked string instrument like a zither) and bass drum. They are a formidable team of multi-instrumentalists which formed by chance at a jam session in a bar in Copenhagen in 2009. Sørensen and Carr were playing when Busk wandered across, joined them, and they gelled so well that they continued to play all night together – and the duo became a trio.

'Kitchen Stories', from their *Rooftop Sessions* album, which was their first to have a worldwide release outside Denmark, is a swirling, pulsing piece that shows off their foot-tapping sound, including a spectacularly speedy end section. There is also a foodie angle to the homespun official video, which is shot in Nikolaj's very Nordic-looking kitchen – the band say the song is about those parties that tend to gravitate towards the kitchen. Like all their music, it has been developed after what they describe as a 'long maturing process'[6] of constant refinement before concert performances or going into the recording studio.

As well as an eclectic sound that ranges from the wistful to the energetically intense, Dreamers' Circus have an open approach to collaboration. They have played with full symphony orchestras and rappers and featured a large brass ensemble and Indian bansuri flautist on their first album, released in 2013, *A Little Symphony*.

'Prelude' from *The Vicorian Kitchen Garden Suite*
1987
Paul Reade (1943-1997)

One of the musical pleasures in life is when you hear a soundtrack for a film or a theme tune for a television programme that really is a perfect fit. Paul Reade's music for the 1987 BBC Two series *The Victorian Kitchen Garden* is certainly on this list, and it won him the Ivor Novello award for best television theme.

The series followed the re-establishment of a virtually abandoned Victorian kitchen garden in the Chilton walled gardens at Leverton in Buckinghamshire. It was hugely popular, helping to explore and recreate rural ways of life that were starting to disappear, and was followed by three further series that took a similar approach: the Victorian kitchen, the Victorian flower garden, and the wartime kitchen and garden.

It was nostalgia television at its finest and Reade's five-movement suite was the ideal accompaniment, a lush, fluid sound, with Emma Johnson leading the way on the clarinet. Reade wrote it for piano and clarinet but it is often performed with a harp and clarinet too, which works very well. The 'Prelude' depicts the break of day and the garden awakening. It has become the most popular but the other movements – 'Spring' (quite a sprightly sound), 'Mists' (very delicate), 'Exotica' (frisky) and 'Summer' (a return to the lushness of the 'Prelude') – are also very evocative. No gardening knowledge is needed to appreciate them!

Reade had a varied career as a musician. He worked at English National Opera as a composer and répétiteur, a kind of musical accompanist and coach. Among his works was an opera for children, *David and Goliath*. He provided themes for another of the BBC's popular history programmes, *Antiques Roadshow*, and the corporation's series *A Tale of Two Cities (1980)* and *Jane Eyre* (1983).

The *Victorian Kitchen Garden Suite* has been a longstanding piece on music exams and those of a certain age will have unwittingly come across Reade's music for children's programmes too. He wrote the theme for *Play School* as well as appearing regularly as one of the resident musicians. He did the same for the surreal cartoon *Ludwig* about a Beethoven-playing walking egg, including arranging the extracts of Beethoven played in each episode, for the colourful *Crystal Tipps and Alistair* and for *The Flumps*.

'Food Glorious Food' from *Oliver!*
1960
Lionel Bart (1930-1999)

Hot sausage and mustard! Cold jelly and custard! Pease pudding and saveloys! A great big steak (fried, roasted or stewed). It's maybe not the most sophisticated of menu options, but it's the award-winning basis of one of the most rousing of songs, 'Food Glorious Food' from the musical *Oliver!*

The song is a barnstorming opening to the show, as the hungry orphans enter the dining room for their usual fine spread of gruel. Instead of this dismal offering the chorus of boys imagine the glorious possibilities of eating three banquets a day, even if it's burned or underdone, to the point of 'in-di-gestion'. It's nothing if not extremely catchy, the work of Lionel Bart who wrote the whole musical including the book, the music and the lyrics.

It's certainly some distance from Charles Dickens's original 1838 novel, simplified and pretty much shorn of its social messages about society and poverty. But although it took some time for Bart to get *Oliver!* staged, it was a smash hit from its first performance in London's West End on 30 June 1960, hugely successful on Broadway (among many awards, Bart received the 1963 Tony award for best original score) and has done well in numerous revivals. It also became a staple for school musical productions thanks to other memorable tunes including the jaunty 'Consider Yourself', 'I'd Do Anything' and the ballad 'As Long as He Needs Me'.

For a man who could not play, write or read music – Bart said the music for *Oliver!* was inspired by thinking of people's gaits – he had a tremendous career and won numerous Ivor Novello awards in the 1950s and 1960s. While *Oliver!* was his greatest success and gave a huge boost to British musical theatre, his CV includes 'Living Doll' for Cliff Richard and the theme tune to the James Bond film *From Russia With Love*.

Bart enjoyed quite a wild life with a range of celebrity friends from Princess Margaret to Judy Garland. Unfortunately, he revelled in the partying side of the 60s rather too much, and his spend, spend, spend, philosophy about money resulted in a lost fortune, not least signing away the rights – and so future payments – to *Oliver!* for a pittance. Happily, when Cameron Mackintosh brought the show back to the West End, he made sure Bart received some of the profits.

'Libiamo ne' lieti calici' ('The Drinking Song') from *La Traviata*
1853
Giuseppe Verdi (1813-1901)

A list of the 10 catchiest opera melodies would definitely include 'The Drinking Song' – 'Libiamo ne' lieti calici' – from Giuseppe Verdi's 1853 opera *La Traviata*, which translates as 'the fallen woman'. One of the most famous opera duets, this bouncy, convivial song with a waltz-like feel comes in the first act of this tragic story about life, love and death. It is a 'brindisi', a song that essentially encourages people to drink and have a good time.

At this point in the action, Violetta, a Parisian courtesan, is throwing a late-night party at her home to celebrate her apparent recovery from illness. Alfredo, a well-off young man, who, much to the disgust of his upper-class family has fallen in love with her, arrives at the gathering and attempts to impress her with his vocal talents.

Let's drink from the joyful cups (*Libiamo ne' lieti calici*), he sings. Let's drink to beauty, to love, and this fleeting moment of fun. Yes, agrees the chorus of guests behind him, let's drink to wine that warms our kisses.

Violetta replies that she is happy to share his happiness and that everything that does not give pleasure is simply folly. Love, she sings, is as fleeting as a flower that flourishes and dies so let's enjoy it while we can. Again, the chorus enthusiastically agrees.

Alfredo and Violetta then sing to each other about fate and the nature of love, ideas that are explored later in the opera. The chorus breaks in for a final time – and the music gets faster and faster to suggest the wine is going down very well – to toast the prospect of drinking through to dawn. Against her better judgement, Violetta finds herself falling in love with Alfredo, but – spoiler alert – things do not end well for her . . .

'The Drinking Song' is one of the opera's showstoppers and works just as well as a stand-alone piece in concerts. Once you hear it, you'll be humming it all week.

Although *La Traviata* is now regarded as a classic of its kind – it's the opera to which Richard Gere's character takes Julia Roberts' in *Pretty Woman* – the audience at its premiere were not wholly impressed, especially at the casting of soprano Fanny Salvini-Donatelli as Violetta whom they felt was too old at 38 to play the role. A more ongoing issue was what some regarded as its morally dubious storyline and there were many calls for a boycott when it opened in England in 1856. *The Times* in particular complained about what it saw as 'the poetry of the brothel'.

'Dance of the Sugar Plum Fairy'
1892
Pyotr Tchaikovsky (1840-1893)

The Nutcracker is many people's first experience of watching ballet, and also likely to be the first in which children perform. It's a great introduction to the dance with an easy-to-follow story, plenty of colourful staging and a memorable score by the Russian composer Pyotr Tchaikovsky. And, because it's usually performed at Christmas time and is family-friendly, it's associated with happy memories.

The plot is based on a story by the German writer E T A Hoffman which was then adapted by Alexandre Dumas, author of *The Three Musketeers* (although the Sugar Plum Fairy doesn't feature at all in these original versions). Set on Christmas Eve, Clara is a young girl celebrating with her family. In a series of, possibly dreamed, adventures she encounters a life-sized nutcracker, does battle with an army of mice, then meets a handsome Prince who takes her to the Land of Sweets where the Sugar Plum Fairy is the ruler. After a series of dances from around the world themed by country, Clara returns home/awakes.

The Sugar Plum Fairy's famous solo dance in Act II is regarded as one of the highlights of the ballet. Ballerinas rightly covet the role even though the Fairy has very little stage time apart from a grand pas de deux near the end. To give the part more substance, productions sometimes experiment with the Fairy's identity, for example turning her into a fantasy version of Clara's mother or the star dancer that Clara dreams of becoming.

The 'Dance of the Sugar Plum Fairy' is also important as it marked the breakthrough into the big time of a new instrument, the celeste or celesta with its unmistakable tinkly bell sound. It actually looks like an upright piano, with keys operating hammers to hit metal bars. As a result, it sounds a bit like a glockenspiel. When Tchaikovsky wrote the ballet, the celeste was very much in its infancy as it had only been invented half a dozen years before by Parisian instrument-maker Auguste Mustel. While it was the composer's idea to use the instrument, the inspiration came from the choreographer of the first production Marius Petipa. He asked for music that would imitate drops of water spurting from a fountain.

Over the next century the celeste became well established in pieces such as Gustav Holst's *The Planets* suite (see page 249) and George Gershwin's *An American in Paris* (see page 197). It is also one of the most popular pieces in Walt Disney's 1940 animated film about music, *Fantasia*, in which colourful fairies dance around a woodland scene, illuminating the flowers for the coming of morning and adding dew to spiders' webs. Most recently, John Williams (see pages 93, 196 and 260) used it to provide the magical sparkle in 'Hedwig's Theme' in the Harry Potter films.

'The Trout'
1817
Franz Schubert (1797-1828)

Despite his untimely death aged just 31, Austrian composer Franz Schubert was impressively prolific. In addition to a dozen symphonies and numerous string quartets, operas, overtures, Masses and piano sonatas, he wrote more than 600 lieder, the German song form that dates back to medieval times. Among them was 'Die Forelle', or 'The Trout', in 1817.

The words come from an 18th-century poem by Christian Friedrich Schubart in which the narrator watches a trout being caught by a fisherman using slightly devious means. There is an allegorical element to the story too as it ends with a moralising warning to young women not to be caught by lusty young men and their 'fishing rods' – think of the trout, it cautions, and, if you see danger, hurry along. In his version, Schubert left out this final verse.

Two years later, Schubert was on a summer walking holiday in the Austrian countryside. Very much a city dweller, he nevertheless had a marvellous time calling his surroundings 'inconceivably beautiful' and happily performing at various spontaneous concerts.

Among those he met during his break was the wealthy music patron Sylvester Paumgartner who commissioned him to write a new work with the specific instruction that Schubert somehow reuse his fish song. The result was Schubert's 'Trout Quintet' (officially the rather less evocative Piano Quintet in A major, D. 667). Written for piano, violin, viola, cello and double bass, it has five movements, with multiple repetitions and variations.

Although it's easy to picture a babbling brook and an energetic trout, it's not really possible to match the quintet to the original story of the poem. However, the music does reflect Schubert's holiday happiness in the fresh air – it's light and bright, upbeat and carefree, very much a feel-good piece, especially as sung by the leading 20th-century singer of Schubert's lieder, the German baritone Dietrich Fischer-Dieskau. Indeed, Schubert was only 22 when he wrote it.

Sadly the quintet was not published during his lifetime and the only people who heard it before his death were his friends in private. Since then, it has become a staple of the chamber music repertoire and lives on in many people's houses in a much shortened format as music played at the end of the wash or dry cycle on Samsung washing and drying machines. It also features several times in Vikram Seth's novel about musicians, *An Equal Music* (as does 'The Lark Ascending', see page 155).

'Le Festin' from *Ratatouille*
2007
Michael Giacchino (1967-)

Disney/Pixar's film *Ratatouille* is one of the studio's most imaginative screenplays, revolving around the character of a young French rat with a spectacular talent for cookery and, after becoming separated from friends and family, his adventures in Paris with a young man making his own way in the world of gastronomy. The score was written by American composer Michael Giacchino who had previously provided the soundtrack for the studio's highly successful 2004 film *The Incredibles* and later worked on its comedy adventure *Up*, for which he won an Academy Award in 2009.

'Le Festin' (the feast) is the charming song that opens the film, a swooping upbeat piece with plenty of joie de vivre that feels as if it comes from the golden age of 20th-century *chanson française*. It was the first piece of music Giacchino wrote for the film, initially as a running theme, but then developed into 'Le Festin'. The French singer-songwriter Camille Dalmais performs the song in French and also dubbed the role of the cook Colette in the French version of the film. It largely follows the main storyline, starting out by declaring that the dreams of lovers are like good wine ('Les rêves des amoureux sont comme le bon vin'), then moving onto Remy's unhappiness with a life of stealing and being hungry, and his hopes of making a fresh start, ending with the delight at being free after a life spent in hiding and the prospect of cooking up a feast ('Le festin est sur mon chemin').

The melody is a recurring element throughout the rest of the lighthearted score. Other soundtrack highlights are 'Remy Drives a

Linguini', complete with harmonica and whistling, 'Dinner Rush', which would not be out of place in an action sequence in an Indiana Jones film, and the final gentleness of 'Anyone Can Cook'.

Giacchino's other film work includes *Doctor Strange* and *Rogue One: A Star Wars Story* and he also has a long history of scoring video games, especially the *Medal of Honor* and *Call of Duty* series. 'Le Festin' and the rest of the Ratatouille soundtrack earned him an Academy Award nomination for Best Original Score and a Grammy Award for Best Score Soundtrack Album.

'Le Festin' has experienced a resurgence, thanks to its use as background music on thousands of TikTok recordings. A special crowd-sourced musical was also performed at the start of 2021 on the site.

EXPLORING NATURE

'The Lark Ascending'
1914
Ralph Vaughan Williams (1872-1958)

He rises and begins to round,
He drops the silver chain of sound
Of many links without a break,
In chirrup, whistle, slur and shake,

For singing till his heaven fills,
'Tis love of earth that he instils,
And ever winging up and up,
Our valley is his golden cup,
And he the wine which overflows
To lift us with him as he goes

Ralph Vaughan Williams wrote these lines, from the 1881 poem 'The Lark Ascending' by George Meredith, on the front of his finished score. Just as Meredith celebrated the bird and its call, so Vaughan Williams conjured up a glorious soaring and swooping musical spectacle.

Like Butterworth and Delius (see pages 158 and 162) he found inspiration in folk songs (though there are no specific examples in 'The Lark Ascending') and felt it was his duty to make his music accessible to the widest possible audience, writing works specifically for amateur and student musicians, as well as writing and arranging many hymns and Christmas carols, even though he was an agnostic. He certainly succeeded with this piece which often tops polls of favourite pieces of classical music. Indeed, it was played during the poignant death scene of Hayley Cropper in *Coronation Street* and actor Peter Sallis –of *Wallace & Gromit* fame – asked to be buried with its score.

Also like many of his fellow composers in the early 20th century, Vaughan Williams's life was marked by war – he served as an officer on the front line in the Royal Army Medical Corps in France - and the piece has been seen as a nostalgic snapshot of the joy of nature before life was irrevocably changed. He wrote 'The Lark Ascending' for violin and piano, but after the First World War came back to it and reworked it for solo violin and orchestra. In this form it has been performed and recorded by some of the finest of our modern violinists including Nicola Benedetti, Jennifer Pike and Nigel Kennedy.

Meredith's poem finishes with these words, matched by the end of what Vaughan Williams called his 'pastoral romance for orchestra' as the violin/lark circles higher and higher until it disappears:

> As he to silence nearer soars,
> Extends the world at wings and dome,
> More spacious making more our home,
> Till lost on his aërial rings
> In light, and then the fancy sings.

'The Cuckoo and the Nightingale'
1739
George Frideric Handel (1685-1759)

The 18th-century German-born but long-term England-resident composer George Handel had a rotten April in 1737. He suffered some kind of stroke or physical breakdown, which prevented him playing the organ with his right hand, just at the time when he and the English public were starting to fall out of love with opera.

Happily, his hand had recovered by the end of the year, but it was still a turning point in Handel's career as he decided to move away from opera to writing oratorios. These still required singers and an orchestra, but were not staged as musical theatre so were less financially worrying. To draw in audiences, Handel often added one of his concertos into the programme.

Among them is 'The Cuckoo and the Nightingale' for organ, string and woodwind. It has four movements and was first heard only a couple of days after he wrote it, in the interval of the premiere of Handel's still popular oratorio, *Israel in Egypt*. It's the second movement, the sprightly 'Allegro', which is the basis for the concerto's name since the organist cleverly replicates the call of the two birds – the cuckoo motif in particular will certainly bring a smile to listeners' faces. It's also an example of early musical quotation since Handel 'samples' a couple of themes from contemporary Italian composer Giovanni Porta's opera *Numitore* and 17th-century German composer Johann Caspar Kerll's *Capriccio sopra il Cucu* which replicates the cuckoo's call on constant repeat.

'The Banks of Green Willow'
1913
George Butterworth (1885-1916)

This lush piece by George Butterworth written for a small orchestra is a marvellously nostalgic evocation of rural England in summertime, with particularly lovely solos for clarinet and oboe. Indeed, Butterworth described it as an 'idyll'.

Butterworth was a passionate collector of traditional folk tunes, often using a phonograph on his regular trips to Sussex in the 1910s where he recorded more than 400 songs from local residents – he was also a keen folk dancer; you can watch him energetically Morris dancing on YouTube. The melody is based on two separate songs. One, which has the same name, he collected from a Mr and Mrs Cranstone of Billingshurst in 1907. It's a terribly sad one about a woman and her baby who follows her beloved sea captain on a voyage but then is thrown into the water. The second is called 'Green Bushes' and starts like this:

> As I was a walking one morning in Spring,
> For to hear the birds whistle and the nightingales sing,
> I saw a young damsel, so sweetly sang she:
> Down by the Green Bushes he thinks to meet me.

It tells the story of a young woman who meets a, perhaps quite rich, young stranger and goes off with him rather than her current boyfriend. Although beautiful, there is also a sense of loss in this piece of Butterworth's music, which mirrors his own story. His promising career as a composer was cut short when he was killed, aged just 31, in August 1916 at the Battle of the Somme; his body never recovered.

He was awarded the Military Cross for his bravery in capturing various trenches, one of which was subsequently named after him on maps of the area.

Writing to Butterworth's father to tell him of the death of his son at the hands of a sniper, his commander Brigadier General Henry Page-Croft described Butterworth as 'a brilliant musician in times of peace and an equally brilliant soldier in times of stress'[7]. As a result, 'The Banks of Green Willow' has become something of an unofficial anthem for all those soldiers whose bodies were never identified and for all the musicians, artists and writers who died during the fighting in the First World War.

'Requiem Aeternam'
2019
Rachel Fuller (1973-)

We have 500 years of music for requiems, all largely following the same pattern of various sections (starting with an 'Introit' and ending with an 'In Paradisum'), and usually sung in Latin. Rachel Fuller's contribution is one of the most unusual since it is a celebration of animals, especially those who are remembered fondly as pets, and aims to give comfort to their owners. As she says: 'The pain we feel is equal to the love we felt for them.'

Having loved animals all her life, growing up particularly with cats, the impetus for her Requiem came when the numerous dogs who lived with her reached old age and gradually died. Within five years, they lost six of them, including Fuller's much-adored Yorkshire terrier Wistle who had slept on her pillow for more than a dozen years. Wistle died the week after the Requiem was completed.

'Requiem Aeternam' is the first piece of the Requiem and the version on the album begins with a live recording of birdsong made by Fuller on her iPhone at the cave in Italy of the patron saint of animals, St Francis of Assisi. St Francis appears elsewhere too, with Alfie Boe singing Psalm 142, the prayer sung by the saint on his deathbed, and often used as a consolation for suffering. Boe also sings the traditional 'Agnus Dei' towards the end of the Requiem. Birds top and tail the 10-track work as it finishes with 'Blackbird' performed by animal-rights supporter Sir Paul McCartney, a new arrangement by musician Martin Batchelar who arranged the other sections as well.

Just as there is a piece of music for every occasion, Fuller hopes her Requiem might be particularly helpful not only when someone has just lost a pet, but further down the road too when they have moments of grief and know that there is something to help them commemorate their lives together.

Profits from the album and concert performances are donated to animal charities and independent shelters because one of the composer's other goals with the music is to raise awareness of animal cruelty and help improve animal welfare.

Fuller is married to Pete Townsend from The Who and previously orchestrated their hit album *Quadrophenia* – Townsend has sometimes performed in the Requiem when it has been performed in a concert version.

'On Hearing the First Cuckoo in Spring'
1912
Frederick Delius (1862-1934)

For a piece of music that so perfectly evokes the English season, 'On Hearing the First Cuckoo in Spring' has a remarkably international pedigree. It was written in 1912 by the Bradford-born Fritz Delius (he changed his name to Frederick in his forties, see page 201) who had Dutch/German parents and was inspired by a Norwegian folk song brought to his attention by the Australian/American composer Percy Grainger, of 'Country Gardens' fame (see page 82). It was first performed in Leipzig under a Hungarian conductor Arthur Nikisch. Indeed, Grainger commented (in a complimentary way) that Delius was not an inventor of new musical ideas, but a genius in building on those of others, likening him to a honey-collector gathering what the worker bees produced.

It's a beautiful piece of pastoral writing, and a favourite of Mark Forrest, who presents his Scala Radio show from his farm on the York-shire Dales; he describes it as 'delightful, pastoral musical poetry written by a Yorkshireman reflecting the anticipation of those fresh arrivals'. The cuckoo's call is depicted by the oboe and clarinet as well as the strings and is quite inconspicuous at first, becoming more persistent as the piece develops.

Like 'The Banks of Green Willow' (see page 158), it is based on a folk song, a Norwegian tune called 'In Ola Valley'. This was arranged by the Norwegian composer Edvard Grieg in his work *19 Norwegian Folk Songs*. In this version, Grieg's depiction of church bells sounds remarkably like the call of the cuckoo, although the words to the song are not at all springlike. Rather, they tell the story of a child being lost forever in a wood. Delius loved Scandinavia in general and Norway in particular. In a 1914 letter to Grainger, Delius wrote: 'Spring always means for me a longing for Norway.'[8] Delius was a close friend of Grieg's and it has been suggested that 'On Hearing the First Cuckoo in Spring' is a tribute to him, five years after his death.

It is a much slower piece as adapted by Delius. However, notes on his early drafts of the score suggest he was initially considering it as much faster and dance-like rather than the more thoughtful speed on which he eventually settled. His final manuscript does not survive, lost in 1912 when it was sent to Germany for publication.

Delius had enjoyed only mixed success at this point in his career, and Grainger suggested that he write something more accessible for a smaller number of players rather than full-scale pieces that required large orchestras. Delius, who had already written music and songs inspired by his trips to Scandinavia, followed his advice. The result was this gorgeous music which continues the association between the arrival of the cuckoo and the coming of spring, a link that had been strong since the Middle Ages. Birdsong continues to be a popular listen today – it can be heard daily on Scala Radio's early morning presenter-less show 'In The Park' from 5am to 7am, which features calming music interspersed with sounds from the natural world.

'Listen to the Grass Grow'
2018
Catrin Finch (1980-)

Classically trained Welsh harpist Catrin Finch – the first Royal Harpist for 130 years when she was appointed in 2000 – and Senegalese kora player Seckou Keita have become one of the most popular world music partnerships, and a particularly excellent live act.

While the harp is a familiar instrument in Europe, the kora – also a stringed instrument that the player plucks – is less well known. It looks a little like a large lute and has around half the number of strings of a harp, Keita using 22. In concerts, the now British-based musician and griot (a West African term for a storyteller, often translated as 'praise singer') tends to use a special double-necked kora tailormade for him by a cousin who is an instrument maker. It's a beautiful instrument, richly covered in beadwork.

'Listen to the Grass Grow' is a perfect example of how the two instruments work together harmoniously. It has a simple melody using just a few chords and was written by Finch to induce a sense of calm in the listener. 'It was the idea of lying down in a field and listening to life,' she says, calling the gentle piece an 'interlude of stillness'.[9]

It comes from their album *Soar*, which takes as its starting point the migration of ospreys, fish-eating raptors not seen in Wales since the 17th century until their recent return. They travel from the area in Wales where Finch was born, thousands of miles to Keita's homeland in West Africa and then back again. The concept runs throughout the album in a wider sense with tracks looking at the idea of colonisation and the enforced migration of slavery. Keita has commented that he empathises with the osprey's freedom of movement and determination to find happiness. 'I've been on the same journey myself,' he says, 'but in a different way.'[10]

The conversation between the two instruments is continued throughout the album, especially in the track 'Bach to Baïsso' which starts with Finch playing part of Johann Sebastian Bach's *Goldberg Variations*, then progresses as Keita joins in with a traditional Senegalese tune type called a 'baisso' on the kora and singing. While 'Listen to the Grass Grow' is an instrumental piece, there is also a beautiful vocal version with the Welsh singer Gwyneth Glyn.

'I Talk to the Wind'
1969
Music by Ian McDonald (1946-),
words by Peter Sinfield (1943-),
performed by King Crimson

The flute has the longest chronicled history of any musical instrument, the earliest examples discovered dating back to roughly 40,000 years ago. So unsurprisingly it has played a central part in the music-making of many cultures around the planet. In the 1960s and 70s, it became a key part of the progressive rock movement, especially in the sound of King Crimson, even though the band members themselves were ambivalent about the 'prog rock' tag.

'I Talk to the Wind' features as the second track on the band's first, and most successful, album, *In the Court of the Crimson King*, released in 1969. 'I talk to the wind,' runs the chorus. 'My words are all carried away.' It's a subdued, slightly melancholic song (about being rather disoriented in the modern world) which begins with multi-instrumentalist Ian McDonald on the flute and features a lovely solo in the middle and at the end. McDonald also played the piano and clarinets on the track, but it's the flute that dominates this almost lullaby. The blissful feel is very much the drifting sound of the 60s, with a noticeable folk influence.

Various recordings of the song exist, including a version with Fairport Convention's Judy Dyble as the vocalist in the pre-King Crimson line-up of the group as Giles, Giles and Fripp, and more recently by Serbian-Canadian musician Dana Gavanski in 2020.

'The Goldfinch'
Antonio Vivaldi (1678-1741)

Antonio Vivaldi's Concerto for Flute in D is known in Italian as *'Il Gardellino'* or 'The Goldfinch' since it mimics what the Royal Society for the Protection of Birds happily describes as its 'delightful liquid twittering song and call'.

Vivaldi was immensely prolific, producing more than 500 concertos for various instruments – including his famous *Four Seasons* for violin, written a few years before 'The Goldfinch' – and two dozen for flute, as well as 40 operas and a huge amount of sacred choral music.

In addition to a career as a busy composer known throughout Europe as well as his native Italy, he was also a gifted violinist. For most of his working life he taught at the Ospedale della Pietà orphanage for abandoned girls in his home city of Venice, and became its musical director in 1716. The orphanage was a hive of musical activity during his period in office, all the more impressive since young women at that time were rarely given a chance to perform in public, far less celebrated to such an extent. Vivaldi's music written for and performed by the children attracted considerable crowds from around the continent.

It is not easy to date Vivaldi's works since he frequently reworked and came back to pieces, but 'The Goldfinch' was the first flute concerto to be published when it came out in 1728 as a set of six. It is a technically challenging piece which would have given his most gifted female pupils the chance to shine in the solo sections but still provided plenty of opportunity for the other girls to display their talents. The solo trademark 'twittering' opens the piece (as opposed to 'The Lark Ascending' (see page 155) where the virtuoso section comes at the end) and the bird-like trills, repetitions, and arpeggios – often accompanied by solo violins which also suggest birdsong – continue throughout. Although written for the flute, it is also frequently performed nowadays on the sopranino recorder, one of the smallest in the recorder family. For those keen to identify goldfinches, look out for small birds with a red and white face, and yellow and black wings.

Concierto de Aranjuez
1939
Joaquín Rodrigo (1901–1999)

Classical compositions often depend on a sporting event or an advert to become labelled as a successful 'crossover' work. Others seem to straddle genres effortlessly without any helping hand. From the outset, Spanish composer Joaquín Rodrigo's guitar concerto has fallen into the second category, appealing to people who simply love music.

Over the last 80 years, it's been recorded numerous times (four by English guitarist Julian Bream alone), given a flamenco treatment by Spanish guitarist Paco de Lucía, a brass band makeover performed by the Grimethorpe Colliery Band in the film *Brassed Off*, and a very special jazz transformation by Miles Davis on his album *Sketches of Spain*. That marvel of the mouth organ Larry Adler (see page 195) has even put his own mark on it. Each version has brought out something new in the composition.

Split into three movements, Rodrigo's intention was to commemorate the flora and fauna in the royal gardens of the country's Bourbon kings in the small city of Aranjuez near Madrid. Fifty years later he was ennobled to become the Marqués de los Jardines de Aranjuez (Marquis of the Gardens of Aranjuez).

Starting quietly and with a slowly unfolding, elegant passion, the strumming builds up in intensity as Rodrigo aims to sum up the essence of the country's heritage. The composer himself said peformers should aim for a sound that suggested the breeze in the tops of trees, the daintiness of a bullfighter's movements, and the strength of a butterfly.

The second movement, the adagio, is probably the most famous, starting with beautiful languid chords before a cor anglais takes over the melody. Rodrigo said that he wrote the concerto partly as a response to the miscarriage of his first child with his wife, Victoria, and this section feels like his personal reaction to tragedy, introspective but not sentimental. The final movement is a more full-bodied dance. Taken altogether, the piece just says 'Spain' and after the Civil War it became something of a national treasure, but one that has spread beyond that country's borders. Classical guitar specialist Craig Ogden estimates he has performed it more than 200 times.

It's a remarkable work, written by a composer who had been blind since the age of three.

Main theme from *Avatar*
2009
James Horner (1953–2015),
performed by The Piano Guys

James Cameron's ground-breaking 2009 science-fiction film set on the beautiful moon of Pandora focuses on the clash between an invasive mining operation and the indigenous Na'vi inhabitants, a culture clash with an ecological angle. The soundtrack for the multi-award-winning movie was written by American composer James Horner, who also provided the score to Cameron's earlier films *Titanic* – for which he won an Academy Award – and *Aliens*.

Both were keen that music should not only play a key part in the film but also be as 'authentic' as possible. To this end, they consulted heavily with American ethnomusicologist Dr Wanda Bryant who helped to create a distinct musical 'culture' for the Na'vi. They started by gathering a huge range of musical sounds from around the world with which audiences were unlikely to be familiar, such as songs from the Central Arctic Inuit, Swedish cattle-herding calls and Persian tahrir singing (a little like yodelling). Instead of focusing on a single form of music, they used inspiration from around 25 different examples – what Bryant calls 'a library of musical elements' – to synthesise into a single style.

As a result, it is entirely unique and other-worldly but not so strange or unfamiliar that it is too much for audiences to get to grips with. It is a soundtrack that does not have the boomingly bombastic feel of an adventure story but is remarkably restrained with many uses of percussion, such as whistles and drumming, and vocal elements as well as traditional string, woodwind and brass instruments.

Horner died in 2015 aged 61 in a plane accident. *Avatar's* producer Jon Landau and Cameron commented in their tribute to him that: 'The beauty and power of *Avatar* lay not just in the superb performances and the visual splendour, but in the music that made us cry and exult along with our characters.'

Although the original soundtrack requires a small orchestra, an elegant cover of the 'Main Theme' track has been recorded by The Piano Guys, Utah-based pianist Jon Schmidt and cellist Steven Sharp Nelson, whose breakthrough came via YouTube. Their version, in which other instruments get a look-in too, retains the soaring elegance of Horner's original.

'Arrival of the Birds' from *The Crimson Wing: The Mystery of the Flamingos*

2008

Written by Jason Swinscoe (1972-), performed by The Cinematic Orchestra

A British group specialising in jazz and electronic music seems a slightly left-field choice for producing the soundtrack to a film about the lives of lesser flamingos in Tanzania. But The Cinematic Orchestra, a musical collective set up in 1999 by DJ Jason Swinscoe, came up trumps after fellow electronic composer Imogen Heap (see page 193) passed on the project.

The 2008 Disney nature documentary *The Crimson Wing: Mystery of the Flamingos* follows the birds as they collect at Lake Natron and the lakes in the Rift Valley in East Africa. We see them being born, growing up, becoming parents and generally struggling to survive in not entirely welcoming conditions as they are attacked by storks and other creatures. The film also has a strong pro-environment anti-pollution message.

It's an emotional and evocative soundtrack with plenty of percussive elements including marimba and castanets as well as the electronic layers. The soundtrack was put together with the help of the string section of the London Metropolitan Orchestra, which has worked on many screen projects, including the *Inspector Morse* theme. The result is a successful blend of the orchestra tradition with a very modern approach.

The music charts the cycle of life from the gentle steps of the flutes in 'Hatching' to the sinister approach of prey in 'Marabou' and 'Hyena'. The stand-out track is 'Arrival of the Birds', which starts with a solo harp before broadening out sweetly with the introduction of the strings and piano to illustrate the climactic entrance of the flamingos. It reappears occasionally throughout the score and, most memorably, a reworked version of it returns later on the soundtrack album, morphing into the more minimalistic 'Transformation'.

If 'Arrival of the Birds' sounds familiar you may have recognised it from the final scene in the Stephen Hawking biopic *The Theory of Everything* (see page 314) – it shares a similar sound to that film's electronic-classical soundtrack written by Icelandic composer Jóhann Jóhannsson. It was also used in the advert for Giorgio Armani's fragrance Acqua de Gioia.

Frozen Planet
2011
George Fenton (1949-)

Even if you are not familiar with George Fenton's name, it's extremely unlikely that you have not heard his music at some time in your life as the breadth of his musical reach is huge – for example, as well as his work on soundtracks, he has composed the jingles to the *One*, *Six* and *Nine O'Clock News* for BBC television, and the themes for the detective series *Bergerac* and *Telly Addicts*. Meanwhile, his impressive film soundtrack CV includes *Gandhi*, *Groundhog Day*, *You've Got Mail*, *The History Boys* and more than a dozen of Ken Loach's films.

But it's his scores for television nature documentaries, in particular those with David Attenborough, that are perhaps his most popular works. Starting with *The Trials of Life* in 1990, he has provided the music for *Life in the Freezer* (1993), *The Blue Planet* (2001), *Planet Earth* (2006) and *Frozen Planet* (2011), which collectively have won a roomful of Ivor Novello, BAFTA and Emmy awards. So popular have these become that Fenton has also developed some of them into concert-length pieces that have been touring around the world for years.

Part of Fenton's skill is that while his music has an immediate emotional effect, it does not compete with the action on screen or intrude in any way, rather, it adds a sense of colour by enriching the narration and images and quickly establishing a mood. It simply adds meaning.

The all-encompassing scope of the programmes means that Fenton's work covers all kinds of action, from tragedy to comedy, taking in hope, courage and loss, narrating the widest possible geographic spread across all continents, in the sea, in the air and on land. So in his work for *Frozen Planet* there is the jollity of 'Surfing Penguins', the menace of 'Elephant Seal Duels' and a powerful sense of driving motion in 'Flying South'. Indeed, there is music here for almost any occasion – a hint of romance in 'Returning seabirds/Albatross Love', something distinctly Christmassy in 'North Pole', and haunting drama in 'Antarctic Mystery'.

TRANSPORT & TRAVEL

Main theme from *The Simpsons*
1989
Danny Elfman (1953-),
performed by the Gomalan Brass Quintet

Whether you're driving your daughter back from shopping for groceries or returning from your day's work at the local nuclear power plant, this is a tune that will bring a smile to your face.

The theme tune to *The Simpsons* written by American composer Danny Elfman has been a popular international earworm since the long-running animated sitcom was first broadcast in 1989. Elfman wrote it after the show's creator, Matt Groening, showed him some initial drawings for the show and asked him to come up with suitable ideas, saying that he wanted something big and bold that promised viewers a great time.

Elfman's first thought was that it should have a retro, *The Flintstones*-like feel. Although unconvinced that it would last beyond a few episodes, he got to work on it immediately in his head as he drove home in his car; by the time he arrived it was largely complete. He jumped out and went straight into his home music studio to write it down.

Over the years it has been adjusted a little by Alf Clausen, another notable American film composer, who provided the score for *Ferris Bueller's Day Off* (1987) and went on to become the main musical composer for *The Simpsons* for more than 25 years. There have been numerous versions by guest artists including Sigur Rós, a particularly raucous one by Sonic Youth, and one by Green Day in *The Simpsons Movie*. Lisa's saxophone solo has undergone numerous changes too. Elfman, who has written more than 100 film scores, has slightly grudgingly admitted that it's probably *The Simpsons* theme tune for which he will be most remembered.

The Gomalan Brass Quintet, whose members come from five different Italian cities, have produced excellent brass cover versions of numerous themes including the *Star Trek* television series, *West Side Story* and *Indiana Jones*. Their recreation of *The Simpsons* theme works really well, recreating the fast and furious fun of the witty original.

'Short Ride in a Fast Machine'
1986
John Adams (1947-)

'Short Ride in a Fast Machine' has all the relentless inevitability of the ticking clock on *Countdown* but with an additional sizeable injection of adrenaline. Its American composer John Adams was inspired to write it when a friend took him for a late night hurtle on the highway in his Ferrari. Adams quite enjoyed it, but acknowledges that it was also an absolutely terrifying experience (especially as his friend wasn't that good a driver).

That sense of almost-out-of-control speed is certainly replicated in the four minutes of 'Short Ride in a Fast Machine', which Adams called a 'fanfare for orchestra'. Although it's written in his trademark minimalist style and ticks all the boxes for repetition, it is far more emotionally dramatic than is normally associated with the genre. Indeed, it has become a piece often used to provide younger listeners with an example of the range of classical music and the sense of energetic fun it can offer.

It starts with the steady beat of the metronomic woodblock which doesn't let up until almost the very end, setting a really stiff pace for the other instruments accompanied by a large percussion section. In come trumpets, clarinets, contrabassoon (providing an unsettling low sound) and synthesisers, loud but still a distant whirling second to the pulse of the woodblock, which Adams described as providing a rhythmic tunnel through which the other instruments must rush. About every minute the music rises almost chaotically to a peak of perpetual motion and then swerves into a new corner at speed. In the final moments, the woodblock suddenly stops and the orchestra feels like it has been released as a trumpet-led fanfare brings us to the chequered flag. It's breathless music, too rapid to be hypnotic and feels like something by Bernard Herrmann from a Hitchcock film (see page 185) or the expansive sound of Aaron Copland (see page 220).

The piece is regularly performed, although the spirited version for four hands on one piano by the sisters Christina and Michelle Naughton is especially worth tracking down online. Adams wrote another 'fanfare for orchestra', 'Tromba Lontana' (distant trumpet). As a companion piece to this frenzied joyride, it is certainly a more mystical listen.

Conductor Sir Simon Rattle has said that Adams' music is a mixture of ecstasy and sadness. With the power of a Ferrari behind it, his 'Short Ride' is music for running fast downhill. Maybe too fast.

'Pleasure Train Polka'
1864
Johann Strauss II (1825-1899)

This is guaranteed to get your toes tapping at the very least and more likely to have you twirling around your kitchen.

Train-inspired waltzes ran in the Strauss family, Vienna's musical dynasty. Johann Strauss the elder (1804–1849) was a keen advocate of the white heat of travel technology. He wrote his pleasant 'Railway Pleasure Waltzes' ('Eisenbahn-Lust Waltzer' in German) to mark the opening of Austria's first steam railway in 1837, operating in the city's suburbs. His son Johann the younger – hailed as the Waltz King (see page 232) – did not share his father's delight in trains and found their speed quite frightening. However, he gave performances in railway station coffee-houses and began writing music for balls celebrating new lines.

Nearly three decades after his father's 'Railway Pleasure Waltzes' and with train travel very much in vogue, Johann II wrote his 'Vergnügungszug' or 'Pleasure Train' polka. Austrian pleasure trains provided magical mystery tours, trips to surprise destinations either close to or miles from Vienna, that became very popular in the later 19th century.

Johann junior composed this highly cheerful piece for the Association of Industrial Societies' Ball in January 1864. It's a spirited dash that includes an actual train horn to sound the departure and returns as an occasional 'warning' as it flies along the tracks through the countryside. Performances often also make full use of percussion, such as triangles, to add to the sense of glittering gallop.

The Johanns were not the only rail composers in the family. Johann II's brother Josef wrote his 'Gruss an München' polka ('Greetings to Munich') for the official opening of the Vienna–Munich line in 1860, and another brother, Eduard, composed the speedy polka 'Bahn Frei!' (Track Clear!) in 1869.

Piano Concerto No. 2
1900
Sergei Rachmaninov (1873-1943)

While his music is often quite intense and sombre, Russian composer Sergei Rachmaninov enjoyed a far from austere lifestyle in Beverly Hills while he was building a career in his adopted US. This included a taste for speedboats, fast cars – especially Loreleys, Packards and Lincolns, which he sometimes took with him on holidays to Europe – and even an early investment in the Sikorsky aviation company, which kept it afloat (and made him vice-president). One of his goals in writing his third piano concerto and then taking it on tour was probably to make enough money to buy a new car. He clearly loved speed and was a keen driver at a time when many wealthy people paid for their own chauffeur rather than took the wheel themselves. Parts of that third concerto are extremely rapid and it has a reputation for being very tricky to play (though having an enormous hand-span made it somewhat easier for Rachmaninov himself to perform).

The third movement of his Piano Concerto No. 2 is also pretty speedy. This was written at a time when his composing career was in something of freefall following a very frosty reception given to his first symphony in 1897. Among those who helped get him through the depression that followed was his doctor Nikolai Dahl whose hypnotherapy techniques Rachmaninov credited with rebuilding his self-esteem and saving his musical name.

Its dramatic third movement, following a stormy first and romantic second, is excitingly express-like and grows to a vigorous climax. The musical marking here is 'risoluto' or 'resolutely'. It's stirring stuff with a real sense of momentum behind it unfolding very naturally with the orchestra.

Many of the elements in the concerto have found fame outside the work. David Lean mined it extensively to use in the soundtrack to his 1945 film *Brief Encounter*, and Eric Carmen happily admitted to using music from the slow second movement for his hit 1975 song 'All By Myself'. The influence on Frank Sinatra's 'Full Moon and Empty Arms' by songwriters Buddy Kaye and Ted Mossman is also very obvious. More recently, composer Bob Chilcott has made a vocal arrangment of the pretty melody of the second movement for The Sixteen choir and orchestra.

Happily, unlike his first symphony, Rachmaninov's Piano Concerto No. 2 was acclaimed as magnificent from its first performance.

Overture from *North by Northwest*
1959
Bernard Herrmann (1911–1975)

There's nothing like writing a review of your own work, but when Bernard Herrmann described his overture to Alfred Hitchcock's film *North by Northwest* as 'a rapid, kaleidoscopic, virtuoso orchestral fandango designed to kick off the exciting rout that follows' he was bang-on.

It's a tremendously flamboyant opening to a film all about movement and travel by car, train and (crop-dusting) plane. Cary Grant stars as the original urbane Mad Men advertising executive caught up in a Cold War case of mistaken identity, murder, spies and suspicious beautiful women who may not be all that they seem.

Naturally, the overture comes right at the start of the film as the clever criss-crossing lines of the opening credits sequence unrolls. It urges us forward with constantly changing rhythms that add to the excitement, spiralling timpani joined by a piccolo and flute, then violins. Next come a xylophone and harps, all at a breakneck speed. It feels like the wild Spanish dance that Herrmann namechecks. Then it all finishes in an elaborate flourish. Herrmann repeated various themes throughout the film and the overture is no different, popping up in different formats at moments of high tension as the cat-and-mouse chase gets underway.

American composer Herrmann was an expert in composing music for movies. He started out in Hollywood with the then *enfant terrible* of films, Orson Welles, before moving on to work closely with Hitchcock on seven films. He provided the storytelling scores for *Vertigo* and *Psycho* as well as *North by Northwest*. The overture was initially intended to accompany the first car chase when Grant's character attempts to escape at high speed despite being much the worse for wear. It works better as the entry to the film and the musical arc is complete as it returns for the final famous sequence on the presidential heads of Mount Rushmore in South Dakota where Grant is again on the run, this time on foot.

This was not how the musical directors at MGM saw the start: they wanted something more lyrical, something that suited the smart New York location where the film's action starts. Instead Herrmann decided to dazzle.

Main theme from *Inspector Morse*
1987
Barrington Pheloung (1954-2019)

The *Inspector Morse* television series, which ran from 1987 to 2000, was absolutely stuffed with music. As a character, Morse loved not just classic cars but classical music, especially opera, so this naturally reflected his interests.

The hypnotic theme music was written by Australian composer Barrington Pheloung who lived and worked in the UK for many years. It was inspired by the rather melancholy temperament of Morse, played by John Thaw, and partly based around the spelling out of his name in Morse code. Both the fictional detective and the composer were fond of puzzles and Pheloung often incorporated little Morse code hints into the music saying things like 'She did it.' In keeping with the detective genre, he included red herring clues too.

As befits a series with episodes lasting two hours, a length that critics wrongly assumed would never be popular with viewers, Pheloung not only wrote the theme tune but all the incidental music too. And then he did the same for the prequel to *Morse – Endeavour –* and its sequel *– Lewis.*

He also selected, arranged and recorded the snippets of classical music which featured regularly in each episode. Pheloung described this as one of the best parts of the job. Whenever Morse is seen listening to a piece of music, it's nearly always one of Pheloung's favourites too, often by Mozart. These sections were recorded exclusively for the television series using the finest players in the world, conducted by Pheloung.

One notable omission was the dramatic German composer Richard Wagner who barely featured despite being Morse's favourite in the original novels by Colin Dexter. Apparently, Pheloung was not a big fan of Wagner and so gradually included less and less of his work as the series progressed.

Morse was quite a cerebral series focusing on a very traditional personality and Pheloung was keen that the music reflect that. The very length of each episode helped him by giving him the opportunity to write longer and more complex sequences of music. He also insisted that the music accompanying the series be an orchestral score rather than something using, for example, synthesisers. This was quite a departure for television music of the period and pretty much unheard of for a detective series. Even at moments of high drama such as car chases Pheloung said he 'aimed for sounds of terror rather than a drum-machine going dodo dodododo'[11] because he didn't want to glamorise violence.

Pheloung had a distinguished career away from *Morse*, composing music for other television series including *Dalziel and Pascoe*, films such as *Hilary and Jackie*, a stage production of *The Graduate*, and the video games *In Cold Blood* and *Broken Sword*.

'Lowlands Away' from *Assassin's Creed IV*
2013
Traditional/Brian Tyler (1972–)

The soundtrack to *Assassin's Creed IV: Black Flag* was written by American composer Brian Tyler. It's an excellent piece of work that runs happily alongside the swashbuckling storyline of 18th-century pirates in the Caribbean. Yet there are some elements which were not Tyler's, a series of 35 sea shanties, collectable as part of the gameplay.

The result is a potent mix consisting of one of the oldest forms of song and the modern technological delights of the video game. It means that the sailors on board your ship the *Jackdaw* can start booming out a range of shanties as they explore the high seas. Some are slightly cheeky, many are upbeat, and a few are quite sentimental. Among this final collection is the haunting 'Lowlands Away'.

'I dreamed a dream the other night,' begins the sailor who tells the story in song of his true love appearing to him dressed all in white like a bride (though in some versions the roles are switched). But her cheeks were wet and she was crying. She said nothing to him but he guesses that she has died – perhaps by drowning – and wakes up to hear the cry 'Lowlands, lowlands away'. There are also versions in which it is sung by a woman about her lost sailor love.

Not all the shanties included in the game were actually sung by sailors, and certainly not at that period, so there is an element of historical inaccuracy. 'Lowlands Away' is a fine rousing shanty, but its origins are murky; it may in fact first have been an Anglo-Scottish ballad. It is only traceable back to the mid-19th century, although it may derive from an older version. 'Lowlands Away' is typical of the genre of shanties that would probably have been sung while raising the anchor, hauling ropes or raising and lowering sails – a solo voice sings the verse and a group joins in for the chorus and occasional whooping. Here, it's sung at quite a slow pace with the chorus an echo of that in 'The Golden Vanity', another marvellous shanty included in *Black Flag*.

Rather than employ sailors to bang out the shanties for the game, the crew consists of four classically trained singers, Nils Brown, Sean Dagher, Michiel Schrey and Clayton Kennedy. However, they were directed to sing badly for parts of the recordings to achieve a greater level of realism. The shanties became a popular part of the game and reached number 3 in iTunes sales in 2013. Sea shanties hit the charts again in 2021 when the craze for them drove a version of 'Wellerman' by Bristol-based folk music band The Longest Johns into the single and classical charts.

One thing is certain, it's absolutely perfect music for loudly singing along to (maybe by yourself, but that's your choice) while driving.

Overture: 'The Hebrides' ('Fingal's Cave') 1830
Felix Mendelssohn (1809-1847)

During the early decades of the 19th century, composers, writers and artists found particular inspiration in nature and dramatic landscape, a development known as the Romantic movement. German composer Felix Mendelssohn was among them, stimulated by a walking holiday in Scotland in 1829 to write this spectacular evocation of the power of the sea. It's officially entitled an overture, although it stands alone rather than being the prelude to an opera or a ballet. 'In order to make you understand how extraordinarily the Hebrides affected me, the following came into my mind there,'[12] he wrote to his family, including the beginning of what became one of his best-known works.

The high point of Mendelssohn's holiday – apart from the seasickness he suffered in reaching it – was a visit by boat to the remote Fingal's Cave on the cliffs of Staffa, an uninhabited island of the Inner Hebrides. His piece, started in fact a couple of days before he reached the site and originally entitled 'Die Einsame Insel' or 'The Lonely Island', depicts the swell and crashing of the waves, the ebb and flow of the sea, a storm and the quiet after it. It is regarded as an early example of the 'tone poem' genre, a piece of music that tries to capture a specific mood rather than tell a definite story.

Mendelssohn finished the first draft just before Christmas 1830. An interesting theory is that he finished it on the only day of the year in which the cave is fully illuminated by sunlight, 16 December, owing to the angle of the sun above the horizon on that date. Not satisfied with the middle section he then tinkered with it for the next two years because he said it lacked '[engine] oil, seagulls and dead fish'. The composer Richard Wagner (see page 216) described the finished piece as a 'masterpiece of a landscape painter of the frst order'.[13] In recent years it has also been used on the soundtracks of the video games *Colony Wars: Vengeance* and the Crash Bandicoot game *Crash Twinsanity*.

Suite One from
Harry Potter and the Cursed Child
2016
Imogen Heap (1977-)

It's the music of John Williams (see page 150), especially his 'Hedwig's Theme', that is most commonly associated with Harry Potter. But that's only part of the wizarding marvel's musical story.

When it came to providing music for the successful West End play *Harry Potter and the Cursed Child*, the directors turned to English composer and multi-instrumentalist Imogen Heap. In fact they turned to her before she knew anything about it as they started experimenting with her previous compositions in workshop rehearsals. It worked so well that Heap – who had not read any of the books – was then asked to come up with something tailor-made for the production.

It wasn't a predictable choice. She had barely any experience in writing for the stage and is best known for her electronic music – she has even devised special gloves which make sounds by gestures – as well as collaborations with such artists as Taylor Swift and Jason Derulo. But her otherworldly sound works very well in what is, after all, a very otherwordly setting. The play is not a musical but it does contain a huge amount of music and very few plays give birth to soundtrack albums.

The score is divided into 42 separate pieces in four sections or suites to match the acts of the two-part play. While some of the music is new, Heap also delved into her back catalogue to rework other pieces to fit the play. But there is deliberately no reference at all to Williams's music for the films.

The Hogwarts Express is the main way that students get to and from the boarding school at the start and end of terms so Suite One begins appropriately with the twinklingly jaunty 'Platform 9¾' (the student wizards' personal platform at King's Cross) and through her signature use of rhythmically layered sounds and ethereal vocalisations introduces us to the grown-up Potter's world. We meet the main characters and experience key moments such as 'Wand Dance' as the pupils at Hogwarts learn their spells. Appropriately 'Platform 9¾' is a reworking of Heap's song 'First Train Home', while 'Wand Dance' started out life originally as the electropop 'Cycle Song' used for a documentary about Bhutan. It's interesting to listen and compare the two. But the up-tempo mood changes as the suite progresses to become a little darker, finishing with the distinctly eery 'Shadows and Spirits'.

You don't need to have seen the play or indeed know anything about the world of Potter to enjoy the music, although that does of course add some extra layers of meaning. 'With over 100 moments of music in the play, the challenge was how to weave them together,' said Heap. 'It is crafted to be listened to in its entirety, taking the listener through different worlds within each suite. I don't know another album like it.'[14] Heap says she was keen to make it work as a stand-alone and remixed the album accordingly, for example adding more trumpets and shortening other pieces like 'Welcome to Hogwarts' (10 minutes on stage, one minute on the album).

'Waltz' from *Genevieve*
1953
Larry Adler (1914-2001)

While there may be some debate about the 20th-century's finest violinist or pianist, when it comes to the mouth organ, there is no doubt it was Larry Adler.

Adler had a very successful career in his home country of America. When George Gershwin heard Adler's rendition of his famous *Rhapsody in Blue*, he said: 'It sounds as if the goddamned thing was written for you', while other major composers such as Ralph Vaughan Williams and Malcolm Arnold (see pages 139, 155 and 15) also wrote pieces specifically for Adler. He was performing into his eighties when he released an album of duets featuring Kate Bush, Sting, Jon Bon Jovi and Elton John.

For all that, he is most famous for the theme tune waltz for the 1953 English film *Genevieve*. This comedy about a veteran car grudge race starred Kenneth More, Kay Kendall, John Gregson and Dinah Sheridan. It's a lovely, swirling piece which conjures up the romantic world of beautiful old cars – a waltz that would be terrific for a routine on *Strictly Come Dancing*.

However, Adler wasn't paid to write it. Instead he was offered the choice of either a depressingly low fee or 2.5% of the film's profits. Against all advice, he took the latter option which paid off when the film became a huge hit. Less happily, when the music was nominated for an Academy Award, Adler received no acknowledgement. He was a victim of the outrageous McCarthyite blacklisting that decimated the Hollywood film industry in the 1940s and 1950s. When *Genevieve* was released in the USA, his name was removed from the credits, a wrong that was only righted in 1986 when his contribution was recognised.

'Flying' from *E.T. the Extra-Terrestrial*
1982
John Williams (1932-)

The scene in Stephen Spielberg's 1982 film *E.T. the Extra-Terrestrial* in which the newly fallen to earth E.T. and the young boy Elliott fly up into the sky is so iconic that Spielberg adopted the image of them 'pedalling' across the face of the Moon as the logo for his Amblin Entertainment production company.

It's impossible to imagine the film without John Williams's 'Flying' theme that accompanies the lurch away from earth for the first time and perfectly represents the excitement of breaking free. This is the joy of flight. It really soars, a gloriously colourful tune, the kind of lush film score that harks back to the early romantic days of the trade and practitioners like Erich Korngold (see page 318). The rhythmic strings provide the best pedalling theme since the dastardly Miss Gulch cycles towards Dorothy's farm in *The Wizard of Oz* (1939) and, as with so much of Williams's music for film, there is plenty of action from the brass section. Spielberg loved the theme from the first moment Williams played it to him on the piano.

If you do find it impossible to separate the 'Flying' music from the film's action, there is a video on YouTube where it is entirely removed from the chase sequence towards the end where the theme reappears. It's a completely different scene, an empty one, without Williams's genius supporting it.

'An American in Paris'
1928
George Gershwin (1898-1937)

'My purpose here is to portray the impressions of an American visitor in Paris as he strolls about the city, listens to the various street noises, and absorbs the French atmosphere.'[15] This is how American composer George Gershwin described 1928 jazz-classical crossover work 'An American in Paris'. It's a gloriously colourful piece in which Gershwin experiments with numerous saxophones within an orchestral context, using the celeste (see page 149), and featuring actual taxi horns.

The horns are central to his depiction of the hustle and bustle of the French capital, appearing in the first 30 seconds of the story about the young tourist who makes his way around town, experiencing a bout of homesickness, but finally relishing the city's uniqueness. On a visit to Paris in March 1928 when his work was not yet finished, Gershwin was struck by the sounds of the horns from the city's taxis, probably Renault Monasix sedans. He went shopping and handpicked his favourite ones.

On his return to America, he brought back boxes of taxi horns and added a section in which four of them are played. For many years they have been played as a kind of scale. But modern musicologists now argue that Gershwin was after a more random, slightly comical, sound which has been misinterpreted because of his ambiguous score markings for the two percussionists. If you listen to early recordings and the most recent ones, you can hear the very different horn sounds.

Gershwin would have been taken aback by the depths of the academic interest in the taxi horns. 'It's not a Beethoven Symphony,' he said. 'It's a humorous piece, nothing solemn about it.'[14]

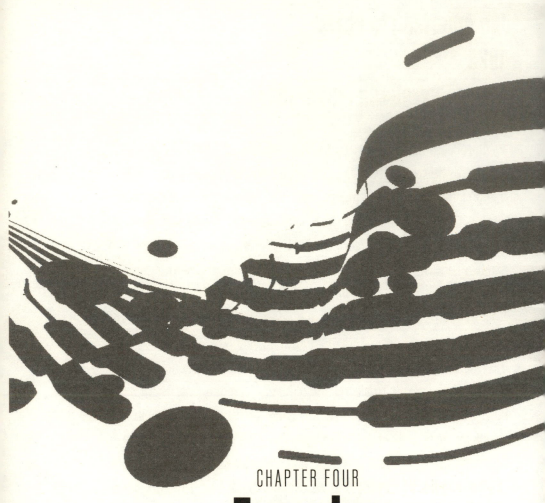

CHAPTER FOUR
Exercise

WALKING
'Walk to the Paradise Garden' Frederick Delius
'The Trojan March' Hector Berlioz
'At the Castle Gate' Jean Sibelius
'The Little Boy in a Castle/A Dove Flew Down from the Elephant'
    Mick Talbot, performed by The Style Council

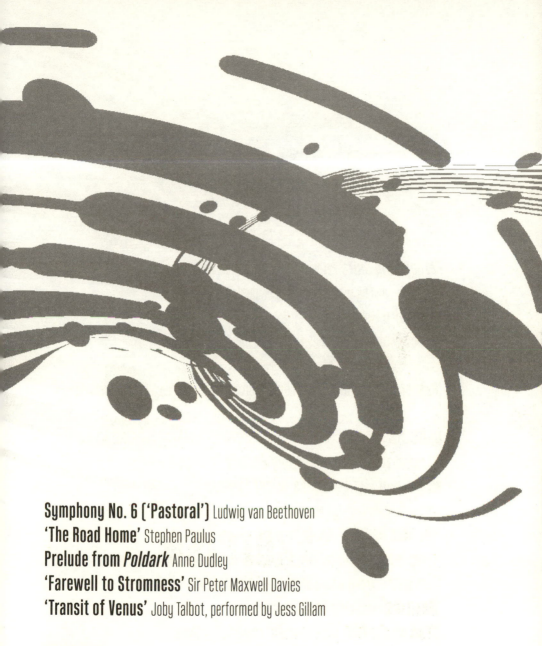

Symphony No. 6 ('Pastoral') Ludwig van Beethoven
'The Road Home' Stephen Paulus
Prelude from _Poldark_ Anne Dudley
'Farewell to Stromness' Sir Peter Maxwell Davies
'Transit of Venus' Joby Talbot, performed by Jess Gillam

RUNNING
'Ride of the Valkyries' Richard Wagner
'Brothers in Arms' from _Halo_ Martin O'Donnell and Michael Salvatori
'Hoe-Down' Aaron Copland

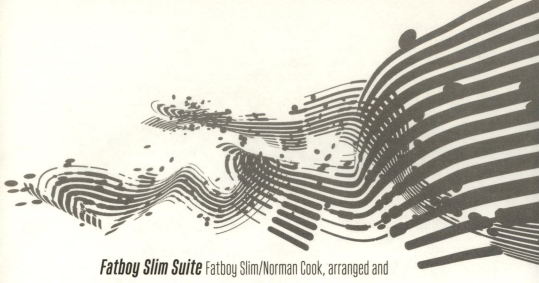

Fatboy Slim Suite Fatboy Slim/Norman Cook, arranged and
performed by the Kaleidoscope Orchestra
'Early Bird' Esko Järvelä
'Dance Monkey' Tones and I/Toni Watson,
performed by the Vitamin String Quartet
'Perpetuum Mobile' Simon Jeffes, performed by The Penguin Cafe Orchestra

DANCING

'Garland Waltz' from *Sleeping Beauty* Pyotr Tchaikovsky
Waltz from *Murder on the Orient Express*
Sir Richard Rodney Bennett
'The Blue Danube' Johann Strauss II
'Telephone' Lady Gaga/Stefani Germanotta, performed by Martynas Levickis
'The Swan' from *The Carnival of the Animals* Camille Saint-Saëns
'Musical Jewellery Box' Stephen Hough
'Maid of the Mill' Traditional, performed by Sam Sweeney
'Kehaar's Theme' from *Watership Down* Angela Morley
'Hungarian Dance No. 5' Johannes Brahms
'Conga del Fuego' Arturo Márquez
'Dances in the Canebrakes' (orchestral version) Florence Price

WALKING

'Walk to the Paradise Garden'
1907
Frederick Delius (1862-1934)

Although this lovely nine-minute wander is a gorgeous piece of music, it's not a ramble to a spectacular National Trust property, more likely to a pub, and a rather rundown one at that.

It appears in Frederick Delius's 1907 opera *A Village Romeo and Juliet*, which is based on a short story by Swiss writer Gottfried Keller with unsurprisingly strong overtones of Shakespeare's famous tragedy. A budding relationship between two young peasants is nipped in the bud by their respective fathers who are arguing over the ownership of a parcel of land. Nevertheless, the young man and woman decide to run away together and at this point in the opera walk from a busy fairground to a not very respectable tavern called the Paradise Garden (things go downhill for the couple from here though they do stay together until the end).

The opera is rarely performed today but the 'Walk to the Paradise Garden' has overcome similar obscurity and is one of Delius's most popular pieces. It comes towards the end of the opera and was written much later than most of the music, largely to cover the scene change from the fair to the pub, and cleverly reuses elements of the music heard in previous scenes.

Despite the heart-rending storyline, this wordless section feels like a walk on a beautiful summer's day. A horn, a bassoon and an oboe set the relaxing scene before the strings breeze in, telling the story of the couple finding some element of peace together in nature despite their struggle. Indeed, this concept is at the core of the opera: life is short but the world is long. The 'Walk' is not all light and fluffy, with overtones of the storm, musically expressed by the violin and oboe, around the pair as the piece reaches various climaxes, emphasising the power of their love. But it still soothes, especially a beautiful flute solo. The piece trails off quietly to indicate their moments of calm are disappearing as the lovers head towards their destiny.

'The Trojan March'
1858
Hector Berlioz (1803-1869)

A massive wooden horse, mass suicide, deathbed curses, the founding of an empire ... French composer Hector Berlioz's mammoth opera *Les Troyens* (*The Trojans*) is nothing if not dramatic.

Berlioz based his plot on Virgil's long epic poem the *Aeneid*, a work he had loved all his life, and he was also heavily influenced by the dramatic art of Shakespeare whom he also venerated. 'Virgil Shakespeareanised' was how Berlioz described *Les Troyens*. Starting with the famous story of Cassandra's prophecy and the fall of Troy, we follow Aeneas as he escapes the city and heads off to found Rome, via Carthage and its doomed Queen Dido. Berlioz was delighted with his work and regarded it as the high point of his career.

Central to the action is the fanfare-like brassy 'March' theme, which epitomises the Trojan 'never say die' spirit. It appears first at the end of Act I when the wooden horse is joyously wheeled into the city and resurfaces throughout the action, including when the Trojans arrive at Carthage in Act III, and at the close of proceedings in Act V as Aeneas sails away to shake hands with destiny – much to the displeasure of the Carthaginians.

Though generally regarded by critics, both now and during Berlioz's lifetime, as a masterpiece *Les Troyens* was not quite such a hit with the public. One problem was the sheer length of it, the five-act opera coming in at a bottom-numbing five hours. As a result, theatres fiddled around with the story, chopping it dramatically – including, much to Berlioz's horror, the 'March' – experimenting with performances over multiple nights, and generally diminishing its impact. It wasn't really until 1957 that it was performed in pretty much its full glory.

A draft manuscript of the 'March', signed by Berlioz, came up for auction in 2017 and was sold for £35,000.

'At the Castle Gate'
1905
Jean Sibelius (1865-1957)

If you're going out for a late night saunter, there's one piece of music that's the perfect fit as you look up to the heavens above . . .

Finnish composer Jean Sibelius wrote the incidental music to Belgian playwright Maurice Maeterlinck's *Pelléas et Mélisande* in 1905. The first section in the story of these doomed lovers caught in a love triangle was called 'At the Castle Gate' by Sibelius who used it as a prelude to Act I, scene 1.

Fast-forward to 1957 when the producers of BBC television's new regular astronomy series *The Sky at Night* are looking for a theme tune to start and end each show. It was the presenter and keen musician Sir Patrick Moore who suggested Sibelius's work. Despite there being no apparent link whatsoever to the programme, it was agreed to use an excerpt from Sibelius's rather overlooked composition. They chose a recently recorded disc by the Royal Philharmonic Orchestra conducted by Sir Thomas Beecham (see page 237) and it has been used ever since. It was first broadcast on 24 April 1957, when Sibelius was still alive, and was a particularly appropriate choice since he was not only inspired by the natural world but also very interested in astronomy. A crater on the planet Mercury and an asteroid have both been named after him.

It's really only the first dramatic early bars of 'At the Castle Gate' that will be familiar to viewers of *The Sky at Night* (which ran for more than five decades) as the dynamic strings section takes centre stage, followed by the woodwind. But the whole piece is equally haunting.

'The Little Boy in a Castle/A Dove Flew Down from the Elephant'
1988
Mick Talbot (1958-),
performed by The Style Council

It takes some bravery for established popular musicians to break away from their signature sound. After the commercial, though not wholly critical, success of their 1987 third album *The Cost of Living*, The Style Council, fronted by Paul Weller, released their next, *Confessions of a Pop Group*, the following summer.

Greeted with some bemusement by fans and critics (though in later years it has been reassessed more favourably), the album is undeniably a game of two halves. Side two is largely The Style Council's recognisable sound. But side one is something rather different and ambitious. Weller admitted that the group did not want to repeat themselves and said they were continually looking to develop.

For a start, side one has its own title, 'The Piano Paintings', which accurately describes the tracks that have a more classically and jazz-inspired feel than side two (Weller described the difference, jokingly but rather unfairly, as side one being for the pensioners and side two for the kids). There is classical harp and a string quartet on the 10-minute 'The Gardener of Eden' track written by Weller, and solo vibraphone on track three, 'The Story of Someone's Shoe', featuring a cappella specialists The Swingle Sisters.

The influence of Erik Satie and Claude Debussy is more evident in the fourth track on side one: 'The Little Boy in a Castle/A Dove Flew

Down from the Elephant' by keyboardist Mick Talbot. It's a deceptively modest little piece for solo piano, a meandering stroll along the keys – ideal for a reflective walk. Talbot has said it has the feel of a film soundtrack snippet.

The executives at the band's label Polydor were not expecting this change in style and the album came at a time when relations between them and the band were deteriorating badly. Weller claims he delivered *Confessions of a Pop Group* to Polydor on a C90 audio cassette.

Symphony No. 6 ('Pastoral')
1808
Ludwig van Beethoven (1770-1827)

The natural world played a central part in the life of Ludwig van Beethoven. Although he lived in Vienna, he disliked the city and in the summer moved to the countryside where he could spend much of his time on daily walks in the woods. 'How glad I am to be able to roam in wood and thicket,' he wrote in a letter to a friend, 'among the trees and flowers and rocks. No one can love the country as I do.' At least in part this was because his increasing deafness was less of a bother in these surroundings where he was interacting with fewer people.

The interesting thing about his Symphony No. 6, known as the 'Pastoral' since it deals specifically with rural life, is that it is not simply a musical depiction of the natural world, but about people and their relationship with it. Beethoven's stated intention was to express the emotions people felt about being in the country rather than just 'painting in sounds'.

He makes this very clear in his titles for each of the symphony's five movements. So the first is 'Awakening of cheerful feelings on arrival in the countryside', the third is 'Merry gathering of country folk' and the fifth is 'Shepherds' song. Cheerful and thankful feelings after the storm'. However, there are also very specific references to nature too – the second movement is called 'Scene by the brook' and the fourth 'Thunder, storm', while birds are mimicked by the flute (nightingale), clarinet (cuckoo) and oboe (quail).

The 'Pastoral' was first performed in 1808 in the same concert with his darker Symphony No. 5 which he wrote at this time; the concert included other music and lasted four hours. It was also used in Walt Disney's film *Fantasia* in which Beethoven's movement titles are followed but replaced with a more mythological theme including frolicking centaurs and unicorns. More recently, the storm section appeared in the 1994 *Immortal Beloved* biopic with Gary Oldman as Beethoven.

'The Road Home'
2002
Stephen Paulus (1949-2014)

'Tell me, where is the road I can call my own' begins Stephen Paulus's short exploration of the universal experience of finding our way in life and the pull of home. The searcher in the first verse describes years of wandering, and in the second hears a voice that could lead them home. This is the voice that appears in the third and final verse offering to provide the signpost back because it says: 'There is no such beauty as where you belong.'

It's written in the style of Sacred Harp singing, a 19th-century Protestant American music tradition, which began in New England and became popular across the country, especially in the Deep South. Instead of all facing in the same direction, the singers would stand in their sections in a square, looking into the middle. The tune comes from the earliest collection of Sacred Harp songs, *The Southern Harmony Songbook*, published in 1835. Originally known as 'Prospect' or 'The Lone Wild Bird', the new lyrics were written to Paulus's commission by his fellow American, the poet and lyricist Michael Dennis Browne with whom he often worked.

It's a soft 'a cappella song', short, simple and striking but not sentimental. Where the original lyrics are in the sacred tradition, 'The Road Home' is contemporary secular choral classic, but in both there is the same pathway from a lack of direction to a final happy ever after.

Prelude from *Poldark*
2015
Anne Dudley (1956-)

Without taking anything away from the actors, it's impossible to imagine the 2019 television series of *Poldark* without its sweeping music. Like the Cornish scenery itself, it's one of the key characters in the drama of 18th-century loves and rivalries. Written by the prolific English composer and pianist Anne Dudley, the music is so much a part of the production that she had to write an incredible 25–30 minutes of it per episode.

Dudley has an exceptionally wide-ranging CV. Classically trained, she has always worked across the musical spectrum, writing short operas as well as working with the likes of Frankie Goes To Hollywood and comedian Bill Bailey, not to mention being a founder member of the 1980s electronic sampling pioneer group Art of Noise. Along the way she has picked up an Academy Award (for *The Full Monty*), a Grammy (for 'Peter Gunn') and an Ivor Novello award, providing music for multiple television hits from *Jeeves and Wooster* to the more recent *The Singapore Grip*.

Her music for *Poldark* really captures the many facets of the series based on the books by Winston Graham and adds to the glorious locations. It's all the more noticeable as there are numerous long landscape shots as the characters walk (and ride) around the countryside, and plenty of gaps between dialogue, allowing her considerable room for emotional manouevre.

Dudley was keen to give the music a genuine Cornish theme and was inspired by the local songs collected in the 19th century by folklorist

Sabine Baring-Gould and Henry Fleetwood Sheppard and published in the book *Songs and Ballads of the West*. Though Dudley did not use any of the actual tunes, she did adopt the feel of the music and a folky atmosphere runs through much of it.

While the whole soundtrack is worth a listen, there are three stand-out tracks. The main theme features the stirring solo of violinist Chris Garrick as a pulsing piano plays underneath. Dudley has described how this represents the resolute and rebellious character of Ross, played by Aidan Turner. The folkishness is perhaps most evident in her simple but moving song 'Medhel an Gwyns' – the Cornish words mean 'soft is the wind'. It was written by Mike O'Connor who specialises in Cornish music and sung virtually unaccompanied by actor Eleanor Tomlinson who played Demelza. The third piece is the 'Prelude', a reworking of the main theme by Dudley for solo piano recorded by the remarkable Chinese pianist Lang Lang, which she calls 'impressionistic' and 'virtuosic'.

'Farewell to Stromness'
1980
Sir Peter Maxwell Davies (1934-2016)

From 2004 to 2014, English composer Sir Peter Maxwell Davies held the prestigious post of Master of the Queen's Music, the musical equivalent of Poet Laureate. He lived on the islands of Hoy and then Sanday in Orkney, and often worked out his compositions in his head while walking around the islands, which he found to be a great inspiration. Maxwell Davies had a deep love of the islands where he cofounded the St Magnus International Festival of music and arts in 1977.

Although very active in encouraging people to enjoy classical music, especially younger listeners, his own compositions were often avant-garde and not always easy to get into. His smooth emotional piano solo 'Farewell to Stromness' is quite the reverse.

It's actually a song of environmental protest, written as part of a collection of pieces called *The Yellow Cake Review* and performed as part of the fight against unsuccessful plans to open a uranium mine close to the Orkney mainland town of Stromness. It's a deliberately evocative soundscape, summing up the purity of the landscape within what sounds like a traditional melody that has been around for centuries. Maxwell Davies talked about his delight at people believing it was so old that the original composer was anonymous, considering this to be a great honour. 'Farewell to Stromness' feels like a tender celebration and has become a very popular piece to be played at funerals, including the composer's own when it was performed by local fiddler Fionn McArthur.

Marked on the music to be played 'At a slow walking pace', the gentle, enchantingly unhurried 'Farewell to Stromness' depicts the tranquil tread of people around the island, leaving their homes for the last time in the event of the mining proposals going ahead. After this leisurely start, the mood surges to a modest peak before calming back down to a sparser finish. Maxwell Davies also loved plainsong chant and there is a similar feeling here of wistful devotion.

It's also a piece favoured by the royal family. Prince Charles and the Duchess of Cornwall selected it to be played, in an arrangement for string orchestra, at their marriage blessing in 2005. It was then, on his father's suggestion, chosen again by Prince William and the Duchess of Cambridge for their wedding in 2011. With the addition of lyrics, it became the eponymous theme tune to the 1983 Channel 4 film *Forever Young*.

'Transit of Venus'
2004
Joby Talbot (1971-),
performed by Jess Gillam (1998-)

Once Around the Sun is a contemplative month-by-month diary of a year by English composer Joby Talbot. Beginning with January's 'A Yellow Disc Rising from the Sea' and ending with December's 'Polarisation', 'Transit of Venus' is the soothing entry for June which he wrote in 20 minutes, the day before its submission deadline. There was indeed a transit of Venus, when the planet passes between the Sun and the Earth, on 9 June 2004.

In this version of 'Transit of Venus' for saxophone, it's played beautifully by one of the young stars of the music world, Jess Gillam. She first heard it aged 10 when her father, who was a big fan of the piece and often played it in his tearooms in the Lake District, gave her a copy. As well as carving out a separate career as a presenter, Gillam's two studio albums, *RISE* and *TIME* (which also depicts the passing of time, but in a single day rather than 365), have both reached No. 1 in the classical charts. She is also passionate about encouraging wider participation in music, launching her Virtual Scratch Orchestra during the 2020 lockdown.

Talbot has also worked in various genres, among them a stint in the pop group The Divine Comedy, producing film soundtracks such as *The Hitchhiker's Guide to the Galaxy* (2005) and writing operas and ballets. He included 'Transit of Venus' in his score for the Royal Ballet's new 2006 production for which he also arranged various tracks by The White Stripes.

RUNNING

'Ride of the Valkyries'
1870
Richard Wagner (1813-1883)

'We'll come in low, out of the rising sun and about a mile out we'll put on the music . . .'[2]

And so he does. Lieutenant Colonel Kilgore, as played by Robert Duvall in the 1979 film *Apocalypse Now*, knows a heart-stopping tune when he hears one. As the military helicopters mass in formation in the air over a small defenceless village in Vietnam, he presses start on his tape recorder and out booms the 'Ride of the Valkyries' to pump up his forces – and dismay the locals – as they move in for the kill.

In fact, it's the exact opposite of how the music is used originally in German composer Richard Wagner's 1870 opera (although Wagner used the term 'stage festival play' in his bid to devise a kind of 'total art') *Die Walküre*. It's the third of four operas that together form *The Ring Cycle*, a complicated story based on medieval epic German poetry and Norse sagas, written by Wagner over more than 25 years. This masterpiece tells of generations of beings of tremendous power, stolen magic rings, problematic sibling relationships and apocalyptic destruction. It's Tolkien meets *Game of Thrones* meets *Star Wars*.

At this point in *Die Walküre*, though, utter destruction is still some way off. The Valkyries enter at the start of Act III riding their winged horses around a high mountain top, belting out their war cry 'Hojotoho!' They are the daughters of Wotan, king of the gods, and are actually returning from a battlefield, lugging the bodies of dead heroic soldiers to Valhalla. All, that is, except Wotan's favourite daughter Brünnhilde who is carrying the body of a woman instead and is about to cause all sorts of trouble . . .

It's hard to think of a more evocative piece of music. The violins start off the ride, quickly spiralling upwards, joined by the cellos to set off a pacy repetitive rhythmn providing a sense of uneasiness. Into this wall of sound comes the large brass section as the tubas, trumpets and trombones put on an electrifying militaristic show, together with three bassoons and the percussion section.

While the 'Ride' is often performed nowadays as an individual piece, for years Wagner refused frequent requests from orchestras to do so until all four 'operas' had been performed in 1876. Although the entire cycle is tremendous, it's a bit long for the average run in the park – just this third 'opera' can last upwards of five hours. Happily, the 'Ride' lasts a more manageable five minutes.

'Brothers in Arms' from *Halo*
2001
Martin O'Donnell (1955-)
and Michael Salvatori (1954-)

With more than a decade of writing successful jingles for television and radio advertisements, composer Martin O'Donnell felt he was ready for an opening that was less specifically commercial, what he described as something 'new and cutting-edge and sort of the Wild West'.[3] And so he moved into composing music for video games.

When O'Donnell was tasked with writing the music to accompany the video game *Halo: Combat Evolved*, his brief was to come up with something to match the Halo scenario. The game is set in the 26th century and players take on the character of a kind of *Six Million Dollar Man* soldier called the Master Chief as he explores the artificial planet of Halo and does battle with extremely aggressive aliens.

The main inspiration for the Halo theme came to O'Donnell, who has also written the music for the *Myth*, *Oni* and *Golem* games, while he was driving to see his co-composer Michael Salvatori. He says he was mulling over 'Yesterday' by The Beatles, and the four irregular phrases between the high and low points of the song.[4] Gradually he morphed it into the monks' Gregorian chant that became such a hit with players (and for which he was also one of the performers).

O'Donnell then began the composing process by laying down tracks on his synthesisers, before adding musicians from the Chicago Symphony and Chicago Lyric Opera Orchestra playing live on top of them, sometimes then removing the original synth element. In the game, the music is linked to the player's actions and changes accordingly.

The full soundtrack album co-composed with Michael Salvatori is made up of 26 tracks, which vary quite considerably from the mystical Gregorian chanting monks in the 'Opening Suite' to the rhythmic drumming of 'Halo' and digital bleeping on 'Alien Corridors'. 'Brothers in Arms' is one of the more pulsating sections, a pounding piece with a decidedly militaristic feel to the crescendo with plenty of snare drum before abruptly heading into a completely new ambient direction with the string section. The actual soundtrack album was rearranged by O'Donnell to make it easier to listen to without reference to the game. O'Donnell described the result as Samuel Barber (see page 286) meets Giorgio Moroder.

'Hoe-Down'
1942
Aaron Copland (1900-1990)

It's the oldest story in the world. Cowgirl meets cowboy. Cowgirl tries to impress cowboy. Cowgirl realises cowboy is a bit of a loser and ends up happily ever after with a much nicer cowboy.

Like John Philip Sousa (see page 303), American composer Aaron Copland wanted to write music that reflected and celebrated his beloved home country and the real people who lived there. He did so using traditional American folk and jazz tunes to add realistic colour. Copland's wide open sound was particularly effective in reproducing the atmosphere of the Old West and its pioneer settlers. One of his most effective compositions was his 1942 ballet *Rodeo*, choreographed by Agnes de Mille who choreographed Rodgers and Hammerstein's musical *Oklahoma!* the following year. She described it as a cowboy-style version of Shakespeare's *The Taming of the Shrew*.

Copland used a number of American folk tunes preserved by music collector Alan Lomax almost without modification in *Rodeo*, his second 'cowboy ballet' after *Billy the Kid* in 1938. Among them is the popular cowboy song 'I Ride an Old Paint'.

The ballet's final movement, the loud and lively 'Hoe-Down', portrays the moment when the cowgirl and cowboy couple finally team up. It's particularly evocative and exciting, notable for its use of percussion including xylophone, woodblock, celesta and whip, with a rim shot on the snare drum used to mimic a gunshot. The violins playing pizzicato add another percussive feel. It starts with, and frequently returns to, the swirling square dance folk tune 'Bonaparte's Retreat' made famous by Kentucky fiddler Bill Stepp (1875–1957). This is then followed by the Scottish-American 'Miss McLeod's Reel', and then the Irish-American 'Gilderoy' on oboe and clarinet. It's a truly American melting pot of sound, exuberant, humorous and uplifting.

Fatboy Slim Suite
2019
Fatboy Slim/Norman Cook (1963-), arranged and performed by the Kaleidoscope Orchestra

It's almost impossible to recapture that moment when a piece of music bowled you over for the first time. Cover versions can go some way towards that, but another option for reliving that first listen is when it is given a thoughtful, complete musical makeover.

This is exactly what the Manchester-based Kaleidoscope Orchestra – mission statement: 'To bridge the gap between Classical and Electronic music'[5] – does with Fatboy Slim's greatest hits, binding them together into the orchestral *Fatboy Slim Suite*. Here are 'Eat, Sleep, Rave, Repeat', 'Praise You' and 'Right Here, Right Now' as you really have never heard them before. A huge strings section, more clarinets and bassoons than are normally associated with the work of Cook, but still the kind of tambourine action to get your body moving. An orchestra, as the group puts it, for the 21st century.

As befits the musical collective's approach, many members of the Kaleidoscope Orchestra are classically trained (its leader, Simmy Singh, was educated at Chetham's and the Royal Northern College of Music) but relish the opportunity to cross musical boundaries. So the orchestra has also collaborated with the likes of Camelphat, Flux Pavilion and the drum and bass group Dr Meaker, as well as producing other orchestral suites using the work of Skrillex and Major Lazer.

Set up in 2011 by Steve Pycroft and David Tagg-Oram, the orchestra also regularly performs live concerts and members put together a series of lockdown session videos during 2020 from their own living rooms when they were unable to perform together in person.

The *Fatboy Slim Suite* provides Norman Cook fans with another way of enjoying his music and offers those who might otherwise dismiss it with a way into appreciating it.

'Early Bird'
2020
Esko Järvelä (1981–), performed by Frigg

The Finnish group Frigg – named after the Norse goddess of fertility – has been so successful it has even had a whole new portmanteau genre named for it, 'nordgrass' (Nordic folk + American bluegrass).

There has been some rotation of band members over the years in this seven-piece. Sister and brother Alina and Esko Järvelä (fiddle) and Petri Prauda (mandolin and the mandolin-like cittern) are the three ever-presents, though fiddlers Tommi Asplund and Tero Hyväluoma have been in the band for 14 years too. The latest recruits are Juho Kivivuori (double bass) and Anssi Salminen (guitar).

Since Frigg's sound is a fusion of classical, folk and world music, it's not surprising that it has such an extensive listenership. It also helps that the group has spent the last 20 years touring extensively, with appearances at Celtic Connections, the Rainforest World Music Festival and Cambridge Folk Festival.

'Early Bird', written by Esko, comes from their 2020 album *Frixx* and like all their songs has a big fiddle sound, the kind of high-energy delight that is such a hit in large festival tents. Plunging and soaring, the fiddles drive the pace which has all the exuberance and delight of a sunny day. It's the very definition of feelgood music.

'Dance Monkey'
2019
Tones and I/Toni Watson (2001-),
performed by the Vitamin String Quartet

Traditionally, a string quartet is made up of two violinists, a cellist and a viola player, one of the most popular classical ensembles for which composers have written pieces over the last 250 years. String quartets often stay together for a long time and, like pop groups, are known by their collective name rather than by the names of their individual members.

The Vitamin String Quartet, or VSQ, based in Los Angeles is a little different. For a start, its makeup of performers is constantly changing, more of a string quartet project than a single group (and with a consequently vast discography). Second, they concentrate on transforming pop music into a string quartet format, what one of its more regular members violinist Tom Tally describes as 'applying rock 'n roll attitude to classical technique'.[6] This means string-based covers of everything from Led Zeppelin to Lana Del Rey.

The VSQ's version of the phenomenally successful hit 'Dance Monkey' by Tones and I is particularly sumptuous. Starting with a simple plucked pizzicato, the song feels fresh and new but still retains the swing of the original version – the violins in the chorus are particularly reminiscent of the sound of jazz genius Stéphane Grappelli's Quintette du Hot Club de France sound of the 1930s and 1940s. The result is a piece that is an ideal fluid rhythmic accompaniment to running but without some of the insistence of the original.

More recently, VSQ has provided a modern classical-style take on the Regency age setting of the Netflix series *Bridgerton*, with Billie Eilish's 'bad guy' and Maroon 5's 'Girls Like You' among those given the VSQ treatment for the television series.

'Perpetuum Mobile'
1987
Simon Jeffes (1949-1997),
performed by The Penguin Cafe Orchestra

The concept of movement that continues and repeats endlessly – *perpetuum mobile* in Latin, 'perpetual motion' in English – may not sound very musically appealing. However many composers from J S Bach (see page 254) to John Adams (see page 179) have written in the genre which requires a repetitive theme to be played throughout, reasonably quickly, and without any pause.

This 'Perpetuum Mobile' was written by guitarist and composer Simon Jeffes for the group he founded, The Penguin Cafe Orchestra, and it appeared on their album *Signs of Life* (1987). It had a truly unique sound, including elements of folk music, world music, minimalism and experimental sounds. 'Telephone and Rubber Band' revolves around a looped telephone engaged tone and a rubber band being twanged, and 'Music for a Found Harmonium' was written for a harmonium Jeffes found abandoned on a Kyoto side street when the group was on tour in Japan.

While the piece doesn't stop, the melody does mutate and change which prevents it from becoming dull. As well as being quite hypnotic, there's also a sense of optimism and excitement about it, the idea of energetically moving forward despite the circular structure of the music. And it's certainly a marvellous backing track to a decent-length run (though maybe not on permanent repeat).

If it sounds familiar, 'Perpetuum Mobile' has been used in the soundtracks to the television series *The Handmaid's Tale* and the film *Mary and Max*, as well as being sampled by Swedish DJ Avicii for his track 'Fade into Darkness'.

DANCING

'Garland Waltz' from *Sleeping Beauty*
1889
Pyotr Tchaikovsky (1840-1893)

The *Grande valse villageoise* is one of Tchaikovsky's most famous pieces of music and comes from his second ballet, *Sleeping Beauty*. Based on the famous Charles Perrault fairy tale, the Russian composer finished it in 1889, 13 years after his first, *Swan Lake*.

The waltz makes an early appearance in the story, during Act 1, which takes place on Princess Aurora's momentous 16th birthday. Everybody is having a jolly time, even if the curse of the evil fairy Carabosse – that on this date Aurora will die after pricking her finger on a spinning wheel – is hanging over her head. Then the princess appears and the villagers carrying their celebratory garlands of flowers perform their special waltz.

It's an energetically festive waltz that captures the whirl and the fun of the communal dance; fans of Tom and Jerry will recognise it from the duo's 1954 cartoon *Mice Follies*. Understandably, given its catchiness, the 1959 Disney animated version of the story uses it several times, sung to lyrics by Sammy Fain and Jack Lawrence – 'I know you, I walked with you once upon a dream' – performed by American actor/opera singer Mary Costa and tenor Bill Shirley. A rather darker but intriguingly captivating version by Lana Del Rey was used as the title music for the 2014 film *Maleficent*.

Waltz from
Murder on the Orient Express
1974
Sir Richard Rodney Bennett (1936-2012)

All the passengers are aboard. The doors are shut. The mist is rising and the train blows its whistle to depart. The instruments and sections of the orchestra individually gather themselves together then build up a head of steam. The train inches forward into a splendid skipping waltz and we're off. Slowly it gathers pace until we're wheeling round and round in a romantic swirl. It's a first-class ticket to glamour.

Jazz pianist, cabaret singer, experimental composer, and writer of symphonies, ballets, operas and film soundtracks, English composer Sir Richard Rodney Bennett was accomplished in so many musical styles. Though he shied away from the massive Hollywood blockbuster, he still scored for some hugely successful films, including *Four Weddings and a Funeral*, the Michael Caine spy story *Billion Dollar Brain* and, perhaps most memorably, *Murder on the Orient Express*. Set in 1935, this classic Agatha Christie adaption had a properly all-star cast featuring the likes of Sean Connery, Ingrid Bergman, Albert Finney (as the Belgian detective Hercule Poirot), Lauren Bacall and John Gielgud. Bennett provided an equally glittering soundtrack that won a BAFTA and was nominated for an Academy Award.

The film's director, Sidney Lumet, initially wanted American musical-theatre marvel Stephen Sondheim to write the score using a blend of Cole Porter and George Gershwin tunes from the era. Sondheim was unavailable but recommended Bennett who watched the film and argued that rather than a thriller it was really an elegant entertainment. Bennett's light touch is announced with a very stylish main titles sequence for piano, played by Bennett himself. He called it 'trashy' but it's very atmospheric, though there are moments of peril too, such as the eerie early kidnapping scene. Considering it's a murder mystery, it's rather an effervescent score echoing the music dance styles of the period including the charleston and tango. The main waltz theme returns regularly and to great effect for the finale. Bennett's use throughout of the harp, flute, glockenspiel and marimba adds light but evocative sparkling touches.

The waltz only lasts a couple of minutes but the 11-minute suite, which is a condensed version of the whole score, is a marvellous longer listen.

'The Blue Danube'
1867
Johann Strauss II (1825-1899)

With a script that was deliberately short on dialogue, Stanley Kubrick wanted to put music right at the centre of his 1968 film *2001: A Space Odyssey*. So naturally he turned to one of the best film composers in the business, Alex North, who had already worked on major productions such as *Spartacus* (also directed by Kubrick), featuring Kirk Douglas, and *Cleopatra* with Elizabeth Taylor. Kubrick quite liked the result – North wrote 40 minutes of music at breakneck speed in a fortnight to meet the deadline – but in the end decided to use none of it.

Instead, he opted to choose a selection of classical music, a mixture of recognised classics and more experimental modern pieces that he had been temporarily using while waiting for North's score to arrive. Some, such as Carl Orff's *Carmina Burana* (see page 308), did not make the final cut, but among those that did was the very hummable 'The Blue Danube' waltz by Johann Strauss II, first performed by the Vienna Men's Choral Association in 1867. Not immediately hailed as a huge success, it only took off after a performance later in the year at the Paris World's Fair, and then in America where Strauss himself conducted thousands of musicians and singers at a concert in Boston. Although lyrics were added very soon after the music was composed, they are rarely sung today.

The full title is 'An der schönen, blauen Donau' or 'On the beautiful blue Danube', inspired by a poem by Austrian poet Karl Beck describing the river's colour. The 10-minute piece starts quietly but memorably with a horn and violins beginning the waltz, then grows and swirls into the main melody. The piece is in fact a series of waltzes which develop this main theme. Kubrick felt it was so appropriate for the film that he used it several times, including an early scene of a space plane's docking procedure with a space station. Initially he had planned to use part of Felix Mendelssohn's *A Midsummer Night's Dream* (see page 120) for this section but the effortless spinning of the dance perfectly mirrors the rotation of the objects in space. It returns right at the end of the film over the credits. Though 'The Blue Danube' was far from unknown at this time, the release of the film certainly brought the waltz to a wider public. In particular it has become a popular encore for the annual New Year's Day concert performed by the Vienna Philharmonic Orchestra.

Alex North knew nothing about Kubrick's change of mind until he attended a pre-premiere screening of the film and was, understandably, none too pleased. There is, though, a happy ending for North as his excellent soundtrack has been recorded and makes an interesting alternative to Kubrick's final choice.

'Telephone'
2009
Lady Gaga/Stefani Germanotta (1986-), performed by Martynas Levickis (1990-)

If you were asked to suggest the best instrument to cover Lady Gaga's smash hit 'Telephone', the accordion is probably not the first to spring to mind. However, Lithuanian accordionist Martynas Levickis, who won *Lietuvos Talentai* (Lithuania's version of *Britain's Got Talent*) in 2011, has produced a fantastic version that really does justice to the original.

The original track, which features Beyoncé, explores Gaga's concern about overwork and suffering from an over-attentive media in her typically spiky signature sound. Martynas retains the power of the original but adds a jaunty swagger that makes it feel like a dance track.

Martynas has a knack of adapting not just classical pieces such as Antonio Vivaldi's *The Four Seasons* for the accordion, but also recent compositions including the James Bond 'Skyfall' theme and Billie Eilish's 'bad guy'. His reworking of 'Telephone' is included on his eponymous album which also features the 'Love Theme' by Ennio Morricone from the film *Cinema Paradiso*. Martynas is changing the public perception of what an accordion can do, helped by the management of Rick Blaskey, who has a successful history of mentoring classical-pop crossover artists including singers Katherine Jenkins and Russell Watson.

If the Martynas version of 'Telephone' rings a bell, you may be thinking of the tango that Anton du Beke and Katie Derham performed in 2015 on *Strictly Come Dancing*. The couple used an arrangement played on the bandoneon, an instrument very similar to the accordion.

'The Swan' from *The Carnival of the Animals* 1886
Camille Saint-Saëns (1835-1921)

Camille Saint-Saëns regarded his *Carnival of the Animals* suite as little more than a *jeu d'esprit*, a humorous zoological collection of 14 short pieces that caricatured a menagerie of animals from galumphing elephants, bouncing kangaroos and stately lions, to pianists and donkeys/critics. In fact, so lacking in seriousness was it, that he did not allow it to be performed in public during his lifetime in case it compromised his stature, except for piece number 13, 'The Swan'.

Written for the cello with piano accompaniment, the elegant portrayal of a gliding swan (the piano represents its unseen feet below the surface), has become part of the staple repertoire of the instrument. The musical marking for it is *andante grazioso*, which means at a graceful walking speed. There is certainly nothing jokey about it and while it appears quite simple, the effortless control needed to play it well requires considerable mastery.

It has also found fame as a three-minute solo ballet performance, choreographed specifically in 1905 for the Russian ballerina Anna Pavlova who danced it thousands of times (a recording of it from 1907 is available online) and whose final words on her deathbed were reportedly: 'Get my swan costume ready.' Russian choreographer Mikhail Fokine who created the piece described it as proof that dance 'could and should satisfy not only the eye, but through the medium of the eye should penetrate the soul'. In his collection of entertaining poems, which are often read alongside performances of the full suite,

Ogden Nash wrote about 'The Swan': 'He looks in the mirror over and over, And claims to have never heard of Pavlova.'[7]

In this ballet version it became known as 'The Dying Swan', depicting the final moments in the bird's life and becoming an influence on how later dancers interpreted the role of Odette in the ballet *Swan Lake*. But in April 2020 during lockdown, principal dancer of the Birmingham Royal Ballet Céline Gittens performed it from her own home – with cellist Antonio Novais and pianist Jonathan Higgins in theirs – in a video that can be enjoyed online. Here, instead of dying, she raises her head at the end to signify optimism in a time of uncertainty.

'Musical Jewellery Box'
1999
Stephen Hough (1961-)

The leading 20th-century conductor Sir Thomas Beecham was among those who believed a piece of music didn't need to be long to be beautiful. Though he was passionate about many great works, he was also keen on what he called 'lollipops', shorter pieces that were performed as encores – something of a sorbet compared to the extravagant feasts of highly complex masterworks. They also make great introductions to classical music for those who want to find out more about it.

British-Australian pianist and composer Stephen Hough has written one of the sweetest such short pieces, 'Musical Jewellery Box', which has all the lightness of a ballet dancer swirling around the top of a little box of delights. It has an innocent sparkle about it, which Hough, himself one of our finest living pianists, conveys enchantingly. If you're looking for heavy 'serious' music, this is not for you. But if you want something fresh and stylish and delicious, it's just right.

'Maid of the Mill'
Traditional
Performed by Sam Sweeney (1989–)

The 'Maid of the Mill' has a long tradition as a traditional Morris dance tune in England – one of many connected with fertility – and as a Scottish country dance. English fiddler Sam Sweeney's take on it is a gently relaxed one, still a jig but more sedate than what you might expect at a bustling ceilidh or when surrounded by fluttering handkerchiefs.

Sweeney's restrained fiddle is matched by a similarly understated piano, played by Dave Mackay, and Jack Rutter on guitar. It's a mellow, catchy sound.

Although a member of folk trio Leveret, Sweeney is enjoying a largely solo career and is a popular performer on the festival circuit. He's modern folk royalty, a member of the hugely popular folk band Bellowhead, which separated amicably in 2016, as well as the inaugural artistic director of the National Folk Youth Ensemble. 'Maid of the Mill' appears on his 2020 album *Unearth Repeat* on which he plays with a four-piece band and which is full of equally elegant but varied toe-tapping tunes.

There are numerous variants of the song/poem including one called 'The Maid Gaed tae the Mill' which was incorporated by Robert Burns (see page 69) in the Scots Musical Museum collection published in 1797. Unlike Sweeney's version, Burns's is suggestively bawdy.

'Kehaar's Theme' from *Watership Down* 1978
Angela Morley (1924-2009)

The 1978 film of Richard Adams's novel about adventurous rabbits, *Watership Down*, has two standout musical pieces. One is the phenomenally successful 'Bright Eyes', written by Mike Batt, sung by Art Garfunkel, and beloved of thousands of primary school choirmasters ever since. The other was the B side of the 'Bright Eyes' single, 'Kehaar's Theme', by English composer Angela Morley.

This soaring waltz is played on the alto saxophone with discreet orchestral background (it's quite short in the film, lasting just 30 seconds, but on the soundtrack album it's offered in its full three-and a-half-minute glory). Most of the soundtrack has a pastoral flavour, which in itself makes 'Kehaar's Theme' stand out. It comes as Kehaar, the strongly accented blackheaded seagull of possibly Norwegian origin, learns to fly again after sustaining an injury and being looked after by the rabbits.

The soundtrack was in fact rather a rush job. Malcolm Williamson was commissioned to supply the music, but pressure of work and ill health meant he had only finished six minutes of the required 90 three weeks before it needed to be finished. In some panic, the film's music director and conductor Marcus Dods approached Morley. She had never read the book and initially, faced with the ridiculous deadline, she was reluctant but agreed after being shown the already completed film.

Morley's work on *Watership Down* was nominated for an Ivor Novello Award and it was also voted one of the 10 best scores of 1978 by the Academy of Motion Picture Arts and Sciences. Indeed, she was the first transgender person nominated for any Academy Award (for her work on *The Little Prince* in 1975) also helping John Williams to orchestrate many of his films including *Star Wars* and *Schindler's List*. Previously, she wrote the theme tune to *Hancock's Half Hour* and was the musical director of the BBC's radio comedy series *The Goon Show* in the 1950s.

'Hungarian Dance No. 5'
1869
Johannes Brahms (1833-1897)

One of the constant features of the works of German composer and pianist Johannes Brahms, whether it was his choral works, one of his symphonies, or his many pieces for piano or violin, was that he was a strong believer in 'absolute music', music for the sake of music, not music that was really 'about' anything. And yet his 'Hungarian Dances' are very definitely about having a good time.

This set of 21 short animated dances is based on Hungarian folk music, originally written by Brahms for the piano. You can actually hear him playing dance number 1 online in an extremely crackly recording from 1889. Brahms loved these traditional tunes, known as *csárdás*, associated with the roadside restaurants and Romani people of the country, and the exotic feel of these dances translated into his most popular compositions. There is even a theory that their jauntiness was a forerunner of the syncopated ragtime music (see page 299).

The one that has become most famous, number 5, is based on the tune 'Bártfai Emlék' by Hungarian composer Béla Kéler. Like many of the others in the series, it starts fast and gets quite frenzied as it sets off on a two-minute whirling ride with the occasional slower section to give you pause for breath. It all culminates in a showstopping finale.

Although written initially for the piano, Brahms worked them up into full orchestral pieces and they work very well with the violin (Brahms was introduced to this style of 'gypsy' music by Hungarian virtuoso Ede Reményi) or banjo taking the piano role. Number 5's sprightliness has also made it a popular light music classic and the Boston Pops Orchestra (see page 16) is among the many that have recorded it.

'Conga del Fuego'
2005
Arturo Márquez (1950-)

The Simón Bolívar Symphony Orchestra of Venezuela has been one of the most exhilarating breaths of fresh air in the classical music world. The orchestra is part of that country's impressive musical project known as 'El Sistema', focusing on nurturing students from poorer backgrounds. Its performance at a Royal Albert Hall concert in London in 2007 under their young conductor Gustavo Dudamel was electrifying. Not only were the young players of the highest quality, but for the second half of their concert they pulled off their traditional black tie dress to reveal multi-coloured tracksuit tops in the colours of the Venezuelan flag, standing up, moving around and indeed off the platform to play, as they ripped excitingly into works by Latin American composers. Among these was Arturo Márquez from Mexico.

Márquez is particularly influenced by the music of his home country, as well as his father who was in a traditional Mexican mariachi band and his grandfather who also played in a folk group. His five-minute 'Conga del Fuego', which translates as 'conga of fire', recorded memorably by the Simón Bolívar orchestra, is a wonderfully thrilling version of the Cuban carnival dance beloved of many parties.

It begins with a tubular bell and quijada (an instrument traditionally made from the jawbone of a donkey) rattling out a pacy beat, joined by rapidly building strings before the whole orchestra breaks out into the conga-kicking action proper. The middle section offers a brief rest from the conga line and features a trumpet solo played in a mariachi style. But then the bell returns and we hurtle again into the wild dancing that leads us to the anticipated fiery end. Throughout, the rhythm and the heavy use of percussion including conga drums drive the piece breathlessly forward.

It's joyful music, music as pure entertainment, the kind of music that impelled those young performers at the end of their concert at the Royal Albert Hall to throw their coloured jackets into the audience like rock stars.

'Dances in the Canebrakes' (orchestral version)
1953
Florence Price (1887-1953)

There is so much more to these three charmingly dreamy dances: 'Nimble Feet', 'Tropical Noon', and 'Silk Hat and Walking Cane', than 10 minutes of attractive music. They were the last major pieces by Price – the first female African-American composer to be given a significant platform for her symphonic work. The dances are typical of her music, which combines the bluesy sweetness of George Gershwin, the rural Americana feel of Aaron Copland, and the ragtime of Scott Joplin, with African-American spirituals. Initially written for piano, the pieces were then orchestrated by another leading African-American composer and conductor, William Grant Still, who was part of the Harlem Renaissance movement of the early 20th century.

These dances are cakewalks, a style developed by slaves on plantations in the American South in the 19th century, which mixed a kind of promenading barn dance with exaggerated high-stepping kicks, but in a graceful and seemingly effortless style. While they were performed for the satisfaction of the plantation owners who presented the winners with a specially decorated cake, they were in fact meant satirically, sending up the style of ballroom dances these same owners so enjoyed. It was, then, a dance of resistance. The 20th-century dance the Lindy Hop is one of its descendants in a much more energetic incarnation.

The term 'canebrake' is also central to understanding these pieces.

Canebrakes were deep groves of all but impenetrable bamboo-like wild sugarcane plants. Slaves were regularly used to clear away these often very sizeable areas to increase the acreage of land under cultivation for planting cotton. But the canebrakes served another purpose. Because of their inaccessibility, slaves used them as either short term or sometimes even permanent hiding places. They were also locations for slaves' parties and meetings, including religious ones.

In her day, Price was well known and wrote and arranged many pieces including choral works and songs which were frequently performed by the renowned African-American singer Marian Anderson (1897–1993). Price's work is now undergoing a resurgence, helped by the chance rediscovery of many of her compositions in 2009 in an abandoned house in Illinois.

CHAPTER FIVE

Moods

PEACEFUL

'Venus, Bringer of Peace' from *The Planets* Gustav Holst

'Pieds-en-L'Air' from *Capriol Suite* Peter Warlock

'Opening' from *Glassworks* Philip Glass

'Contrapunctus I' from *The Art of Fugue* Johann Sebastian Bach

'Kashmiri Song' Music by Amy Woodforde-Finden, words by Violet Nicolson

'In Paradisum' from *Requiem* Gabriel Fauré

'ekki hugsa' Ólafur Arnalds

'De Profundis' performed by Nova Schola Gregoriana

'Lara's Theme' from *Doctor Zhivago* Maurice Jarre

'Berceuse aux Étoiles' Jacques Ibert
'Avril 14th' Aphex Twin

SAD

'Un Bel dì Vedremo' from *Madama Butterfly* Giacomo Puccini
'Dolorosa' from *Stabat Mater* Giovanni Pergolesi
'Pie Jesu' from *Requiem* Andrew Lloyd Webber
'Pavane pour une Infante Défunte' Maurice Ravel
'Music for a While' Henry Purcell
'Adagio' from Cello Concerto in E minor Sir Edward Elgar
Main theme from *Schindler's List* John Williams
'Elegia' New Order
'Cantus in memory of Benjamin Britten' Arvo Pärt
'Bathroom dance' from *Joker* Hildur Guðnadóttir
Main theme from *The English Patient* Gabriel Yared
'Adagio for Strings' Samuel Barber

INSPIRATIONAL

'Fugue' from *The Young Person's Guide to the Orchestra*
  Benjamin Britten

'Tonight' from *West Side Story* Leonard Bernstein, lyrics by Stephen Sondheim

'The Ecstasy of Gold' from *The Good, the Bad and the Ugly* Ennio Morricone

'Maestoso' finale from the 'Organ Symphony' Camille Saint-Saëns

Opening toccata to *Orfeo* Claudio Monteverdi

'O Radiant Dawn' from *The Strathclyde Motets* James MacMillan

'Maple Leaf Rag' Scott Joplin

'Attaboy' Stuart Duncan, Yo-Yo Ma, Edgar Meyer and Chris Thile

'The Liberty Bell March' John Philip Sousa

'I Was Glad' Sir Hubert Parry

'Heart-Shaped Box' Kurt Cobain, covered by
  Hackney Colliery Band

'Fortune Plango Vulnera' from *Carmina Burana* Carl Orff

'Finding the Pattern' from *Everybody's Gone To the Rapture*
  Jessica Curry

Symphony No. 3 ('Eroica') Ludwig van Beethoven

'Cambridge, 1963' from *The Theory of Everything*
  Jóhann Jóhannsson

'Baba Yetu' from *Civilization IV* Christopher Tin

Main theme from *The Adventures of Robin Hood*
  Erich Korngold

PEACEFUL

'Venus, Bringer of Peace' from *The Planets* 1918

Gustav Holst (1874-1934)

Having decided to change career from professional trombonist to composer, Gustav Holst found it hard to make a name for himself. The turning point came on a walking holiday in Majorca with the lyricist and hymn writer Clifford Bax when his friend introduced him to the study of astrology. This piqued Holst's interest and he began a project to write several connected pieces, some original work and some recycled from previous projects, which eventually became *The Planets* (the working title was the far less glamorous *Seven Pieces for Large Orchestra*).

Rather than follow the characterisations of the Roman gods, Holst preferred to name each of the seven movements depicting our solar system along astrological and psychological lines. Mars represents war (and inspired John Williams's 'The Imperial March' in *Star Wars*), Jupiter jollity and Saturn (Holst's personal favourite) old age. On this basis, Venus stands for peace, rebuffing its predecessor.

As the second piece in the suite, 'Venus' is sandwiched between the militaristic 'Mars' and the jaunty 'Mercury'. The music is a strong contrast to both, played at a slower pace and creating a relaxing atmosphere, but one with slightly enigmatic overtones. Venus's arrival is heralded with a solo horn, joined by oboes and flutes, with the harp, celeste and glockenspiel providing that other-worldly sensation alongside a glorious solo violin. In the programme notes for one of its earliest performances in 1919, Holst wrote: 'The whole of this movement is pervaded by the serenity of a world which nothing seems able to disturb. The mood is unmistakably mystical and the hero may indeed imagine himself contemplating the twinkling stars on a still night.'[1]

It's interesting that Holst calls it 'mystical', setting it up as a companion piece to the final section of the suite when 'Neptune the mystic', fades imperceptibly into the distance. In later life, Holst felt his work was a little bloodless and lacking in warmth, but his fellow composer Ralph Vaughan Williams described it rather as 'supra-human' and added that 'his music reaches into the unknown, but it never loses touch with humanity'.

Though Holst had other minor successes – his setting of 'In the Bleak Midwinter' is a well-liked Christmas favourite – *The Planets* is by far his most popular work and there are many recordings of the suite. It usually lasts around 50 minutes but when Holst conducted the London Symphony Orchestra in one of the earliest recordings in the 1920s he pushes it along at quite a lick and it comes in ten minutes shorter.

The depiction of the planets in Holst's suite bear no resemblance to their actual physical state. 'Fiery' Mars is actually reasonably hospitable, while 'fragrant' Venus is hellishly hot and suffers from sulphuric acid rain.

'Pieds-en-L'Air' from *Capriol Suite*
1926
Peter Warlock (1894-1930)

Despite his conventional English family background and formal education at Eton and Oxford, Peter Warlock did not live the life of a standard classical composer. He led a pretty wild, bohemian life, scandalising villagers with his sexual antics in the various places where he rented cottages, heedlessly fathering children (probably including the art critic Brian Sewell), and changing his name, which was originally Philip Heseltine, after he became interested in magic and the occult. His lovely Christmas song 'Bethlehem Down' is a beautifully tender modern carol but was written solely to pay for a monumental festive drinking session with friends in 1927.

However, Warlock's stormy life is not reflected in his music. His early music hero and mentor was the lyrical composer Frederick Delius (see pages 162 and 201) for whose 60th birthday Warlock wrote his captivating 'Serenade for Strings'. He also had a lifelong interest in medieval and Renaissance music, which he wrote about as a journalist and helped to revive. His best-known work, the Capriol Suite, was inspired by tunes in a 16th-century guide to dances called *Orchésographie* by French clergyman Jehan Tabourot, who co-incidentally also wrote under a pseudonym. The six sections Warlock composed only last around ten minutes in total and are named after dances, including the 'Basse-Danse', 'Pavane', 'Tordion' and 'Bransles'.

The prettiest of them is 'Pieds-en-L'Air', which, despite being a step in quite lively dances (it means 'feet in the air'), is here given a very lyrical treatment – the musical marking is 'Andante tranquillo' or 'at a calm walking pace'. The feel of gliding is in marked contrast to the stately feel of the others, especially the final sparkling movement, 'Mattachins', which is a sword dance marked 'Allegro con brio' or 'fast with spirit'.

The suite began life as a piano duet but Warlock later reworked it for strings and then full orchestra.

'Opening' from *Glassworks*
1981
Philip Glass (1937-)

Minimalism emerged in the 1960s and 70s when composers such as Michael Nyman and Steve Reich began using a lot of repetition, limited notes and minor circling variations in their music. One of the most famous names associated with the movement, even though he's not so keen on the term, is American composer Philip Glass.

Glass is also not keen on pigeon-holing his music. He's written violin concertos, operas, film scores (notably for his BAFTA-winning *The Hours* and the ground-breaking 1982 *Koyaanisqatsi*), collaborated with Aphex Twin (see page 265) and David Byrne, and his work has featured in several video games, including *Grand Theft Auto IV* and *Assassins Creed*. 'Opening', which is typical of his work, comes from his 1982 six-track album *Glassworks* which Glass wrote specifically 'to introduce my music to a more general audience'[2] that was not familiar with classical music. Indeed, he created a mix specifically for cassette to be listened to on Walkmans when they still represented the white heat of music technology.

Unlike much of the album, which makes extensive use of saxophones and synthesiser to produce a more hectic sound, 'Opening' is a work for solo piano. This brooding, stripped-down, first track lasts 6 minutes and 24 seconds and, despite its minimalist nature, still feels purposeful. Glass said he placed it first on the album to establish an intimate atmosphere with the listener from the word go. The theme returns in the final track on the album, 'Closing'. It's just the thing if you're looking to settle down into a gentle trance.

'Contrapunctus I' from *The Art of Fugue* 1750
Johann Sebastian Bach (1685-1750)

The celebrated Canadian pianist Glenn Gould said that, cast away on a desert island and able to listen to the work of only one composer, he would choose Johann Sebastian Bach. 'To Bach,' remarked conductor and composer Leonard Bernstein, 'notes were not just sounds but the very stuff of creation.'[3] There's certainly a case to be made for saying that as a composer Bach was the Greatest Of All Time.

Published posthumously in 1751, one of his final masterpieces as his health and eyesight were starting to deteriorate was *Die Kunst der Fuge* or *The Art of Fugue*. A fugue is essentially a number of variations on a very short theme made up of the same few notes. These are developed in a variety of creative ways – even played backwards or upside down – as instruments or voices weave in and out to create different moods. It's not exactly a maths challenge but it's certainly something of a musical experiment. And when it works well, it's a sensational listen. Bach's works very well.

There are 18 sections or movements in *The Art of Fugue*. It starts with 'Contrapunctus I', which lays out the very first building blocks of what is to follow. The theme becomes increasingly elaborate, sometimes even quite jazzy, but here it's pure and simple.

The work has been much debated by musicologists over the centuries. Bach didn't specify exactly which instrument(s) it should be played on, though the organ and harpsichord are frontrunners. While these days it's commonly performed on the piano, it has been cleverly arranged for saxophone ensemble, string quartet and brass. The

Swingle Singers have even recorded a rather glitzy version for voice; it's a seriously clever work but it doesn't need to be performed seriously.

Another mystery is that it is incomplete. The final section, 'Contrapunctus XIV', just trails off. One theory is that Bach did this deliberately, leaving later musicians to provide their own resolution to the puzzle. And finally, it's not even clear whether he wrote it to be performed publicly (it was only done so for the first time in 1922, nearly 200 years after his death) or just as an intellectual workout to train himself and help stimulate other musicians. None of this really matters. It's simply a masterpiece.

If you find *The Art of Fugue* delicately addictive, investigate Bach's *The Well-Tempered Clavier* where he also plays imaginatively with the idea of fugue.

'Kashmiri Song'
1902
Music by Amy Woodforde-Finden (1860-1919), words by Violet Nicolson (1865-1904)

> Pale hands I loved beside the Shalimar
> Where are you now? Who lies beneath your spell?

These words from 'Kashmiri Song' by Violet Nicolson, writing under the nom de plume of Laurence Hope, provided songwriter Amy Woodforde-Finden with the basis for her first huge hit.

Both Woodforde-Finden and Nicolson were influenced by the music and poetry of India where they lived around the same time, being married to English army officers of the Raj. Nicolson's romantic but often quite sad poems were very popular and 'Kashmiri Song' appears in her 1902 collection *India's Love Lyrics*, the Shalimar a reference to the gardens in either Kashmir or Lahore. Woodforde-Finden's sentimental ballad was published in 1902 and it immediately became a symbol of the 'exotic Orient' and hugely popular over the next 40 years.

Major artists, such as Australian singer Peter Dawson, recorded the song, it appeared in various films including *Hers to Hold* (1943) sung by leading star of 1940s musicals Deanna Durbin, and it frequently found its way into many books from Bertie Wooster singing it in the bath in *Jeeves and the Feudal Spirit* (1954) to Vikram Seth's blockbuster *A Suitable Boy* (1994).

Since then it has been slightly forgotten but it's a memorably touching song about a lost love, usually performed by a tenor, and was included by cellist Julian Lloyd Webber on his 2006 album *Unexpected Songs*, a collection of songs from a bygone age.

'In Paradisum' from *Requiem*
1888
Gabriel Fauré (1845-1924)

French composer Gabriel Fauré had no strong Catholic beliefs. In fact he used to nip out for a cigarette during sermons at his local church where he played the organ. So while most requiems are, understandably, fairly traditional and solemn affairs, it's not surprising that the one he composed in the late 1880s is rather lighter.

Instead of focusing on the more upsetting and dramatic elements of a requiem, Fauré opted for a gentler sound and concentrates more on the possibility of a better afterlife. This is also reflected in the Latin texts he used, dropping almost entirely the typical fiery 'Dies irae' section about the Day of Judgement and closing the work with 'In Paradisum', usually sung at burials rather than funeral services. 'In paradisum deducant te Angeli,' it begins, 'May the angels lead you into paradise, may choirs of angels receive you and like Lazarus, once a poor man, may you have eternal rest.'

In short, it's a beautifully peaceful requiem, rooted in Christian faith but lacking in torment, and his three-minute 'In Paradisum' is a perfect ending to it. It's a depiction of nothing less than a purgatory-free paradise, a musical solace led by the organ and the choir's sopranos (including a soloist) before the male singers join in and they reach a contemplative ending together. It's certainly in line with Fauré's own views on death which he regarded as 'a happy deliverance. . . rather than a painful experience'[4] on the way to eternal rest.

Although he said he wrote it purely for musical pleasure, Fauré's *Requiem* may also have been partly conceived as a tribute to his father, who died in 1885. His mother died while he was writing it and it was first performed at her funeral in January 1888, including the 'In Paradisum'. In 1924, it was also performed at Fauré's own funeral.

'ekki hugsa'
2018
Ólafur Arnalds (1986-)

Ólafur Arnalds's signature layered electronic sound will be familiar to viewers of the ITV crime drama series *Broadchurch* for which he composed the unsettling credits theme and score (and won a BAFTA in the process). But several years after his *Broadchurch* work, he experienced something of a musical epiphany.

'The phrase "ekki hugsa" was handed to me on a piece of paper by a stranger once,' tweeted the Icelandic multi-instrumentalist and ambient electronic music composer in 2019. 'I went home and put it on my wall. It's been my mantra ever since. It means "don't think".'[5]

Arnalds took an interesting approach to this advice with his 2018 album *re:member* which features the track 'ekki hugsa'. It was composed using his bespoke musical software system called Stratus – when he played a note on his piano, it triggered two other self-playing pianos to play a different note. The unexpected effect in 'ekki hugsa', which adds a cello into the minimalist mix, is not robotic, but it is pulsatingly hypnotic. The same software was used to create the album's cover artwork, a series of dots in a rough square that correspond to the notes played on the title track.

The official video of the song develops this concept a stage further, mixing contemporary and traditional dance steps performed by young dancers. 'The video is about not overthinking and getting lost in a moment,' says Arnalds. 'When you turn off the noise in your brain so much creativity can be discovered inside of yourself.'

'De Profundis'
Traditional
Performed by Nova Schola Gregoriana

Gregorian chant has a 1,000-year-old history as a central part of the church's liturgy, accompanying the daily services from the morning matins to the evening compline without any additional instrumentation.

Over the last 40 years, Gregorian chant has also made a surprisingly significant impact on the music charts. In 1990, German group Enigma made use of the 'Procedamus in pace!' chant, 'enlivened' by a hip-hop beat and synthesiser to produce their distinctly non-ecclesiastical chill-out track 'Sadeness'. Four years later, the *Chant* album by the Benedictine monks of Santo Domingo de Silos in Spain was promoted as a remedy to the aggravations of modern life. It went double platinum in the US and sold six million copies around the world before the monks happily escaped the glare of the media.

During the lockdowns of 2020 and 2021 the Benedictine nuns of the Abbey of Notre-Dame de Fidélité in Jouques, near Aix-en Provence in France, released a huge number of Gregorian chants, which they sang live as part of their daily services. Similarly, sisters of the Poor Clares of Arundel based at a convent in West Sussex found success with their chant album *Light for the World*, with light accompaniment rather than vocal only.

One of the finest recordings is *Adorate deum* by the Italian group Nova Schola Gregoriana in 1993, which specialises in researching and performing chants. It also has the added atmospheric benefit of being recorded in the Church of the Nativity of the Blessed Virgin Mary in Mantua, Italy. Their 'De Profundis', which comes from Psalm 130 ('De profundis clamavi ad te, Domine'/'Out of the depths I cry to you, O Lord') and is traditionally sung on the 23rd day of Pentecost, is a typical example of the chant's simple and timeless beauty.

'Lara's Theme'
from *Doctor Zhivago*
1965
Maurice Jarre (1924-2009)

There are three leading characters in the 1965 romantic Russian civil war drama *Doctor Zhivago*, based on the novel of the same name by Boris Pasternak. Omar Sharif is the dashing poet Yuri, Julie Christie is the nurse he loves, and centre-stage throughout is the balalaika.

The score for the film was written by French composer Maurice Jarre who had previously worked with the film's director David Lean on *Lawrence of Arabia*. Initially, Lean had wanted to use a Russian folk song to represent Lara but when he was unable to find the copyright holder he asked Jarre to provide an alternative. Lean turned down Jarre's first offering that he had written for the piano, found his second attempt too sad and his third too fast. At this point he suggested that Jarre should think about something with a wider appeal, 'forget about Russia'[6] and take his girlfriend to the Santa Monica Mountains where he should write her a love song.

'Lara's Theme' was the result of this trip, which Jarre then set for the balalaika – a traditional Russian instrument resembling a long-necked lute with a triangular body – to add a folksy Russian touch. For an additional element of authenticity, it was recorded by musicians from various Russian Orthodox churches in Los Angeles who took a while to learn the piece since they couldn't read music.

There is actually no single 'Lara's Theme' on the soundtrack album where the balalaikas are joined by their similar cousins the domra and the mandolin. It's first heard in the long 'Overture' and 'Main Theme' at the start, then frequently throughout when Lara appears, especially in the scene later in the film when the seasons change. It returns at the end in a very upbeat and optimistic fashion. It's a very memorable piece of music but if you listen to the soundtrack album straight through, you do get a lot of variations on the same theme.

Soon after the film's release, Paul Francis Webster added lyrics to 'Lara's Theme', which became 'Somewhere My Love' and was a hit single for American singer Connie Francis and the relentlessly perky but not very wintry Ray Conniff Singers. The tune also pops up at the beginning of the 1977 James Bond film *The Spy Who Loved Me* when a spy's transmitter disguised as a music box pipes up.

Although initially the film was not universally loved, Jarre won a Golden Globe and an Academy Award for his original score.

'Berceuse aux Étoiles'
1943
Jacques Ibert (1890-1962)

A 'berceuse' is a lullaby in French. But the soothing, rocking feel to French composer Jacques Ibert's 'Berceuse aux Étoiles' ('Lullaby to the stars') for piano can be enjoyed by anyone of any age. Ibert was not a follower of any particular 20th-century musical movement. He was important enough to run the Paris Opera, and happily wrote original music for Gene Kelly's 1956 movie *Invitation to the Dance*. Out of favour with the Vichy government in France during the Second World War, he wrote his perky *Petite Suite en 15 Images*. His 'berceuse' is the fourth of these 15 charming small piano 'pictures', and it is 100 seconds of serenity.

'Avril 14th'
2001
Aphex Twin (1971-)

Richard D James, who more famously goes by his performing name of Aphex Twin, is best known for his instrumental electronic and ambient music. And so the sweet two-minute track 'Avril 14th' on his 2001 double album *Drukqs* was something of a departure.

'Avril 14th' is a gentle solo piano piece, a world away from Aphex Twin's often chaotic sound. It's actually recorded on a Yamaha Disklavier, a piano that is played via an electronic mechanism using MIDI (Music Instrument Digital Interface) computer data. The absence of an actual human pianist adds an otherworldliness to the result. In 2018, Aphex Twin released a version played at half speed which is fascinating but, unsurprisingly, feels very, very slow indeed.

It appears in Sofia Coppola's 2006 film *Marie Antoinette* in a scene where the Queen goes for a walk, and Chris Morris chose it to play over the final scene of his satirical 2010 film *Four Lions* because of its melancholic feel. James recorded a special version of it specifically for the film. More controversially, it appears on 'Blame Game' by Kanye West whom James claims tried to avoid payment for its use.

Why James picked Avril 14th as its name is unclear but there is some speculation that it may be related to the strangely large number of tragedies that have occurred on 14 April in history, including Abraham Lincoln's assassination, the *Titanic* hitting an iceberg, and numerous meteorological disasters.

SAD

'Un Bel dì Vedremo' from *Madama Butterfly*
1904
Giacomo Puccini (1858-1924)

Lieutenant Pinkerton, a US naval officer stationed in Japan, rents a house that comes with three servants and a geisha, Cio-Cio San ('butterfly' in English). She falls in love with him, converts to Christianity and the couple are married, despite Pinkerton's admission to a friend that he is keen to marry an American woman. Soon afterwards, Pinkerton is reassigned to a post outside Japan. Three years later, Butterfly and their young child are still waiting for his return . . .

At this point in Puccini's opera, Butterfly sings one of the most famous arias in opera, 'Un bel dì vedremo' ('One fine day we shall see'). Despite his long absence and lack of contact (and the gloomy outlook of her servant Suzuki), she still has complete faith in Pinkerton and sings of how one day from her house on the hill she will spot the ship slowly coming into port, and watch him climb up the hill to be reunited with her.

The opera is not a blockbuster in terms of spectacle and large choruses. It's a simple plot and this is a hugely affecting moment, the emotional centre of the whole opera that requires the soprano singing the part to show her acting range too. It has the quietest of beautiful starts as Butterfly and a violin sing of her hopes, rising to a climax when the two lovers are destined to meet again and, in Butterfly's eyes, be together forever. The mixture of restrained patience erupting into blind passion means it's not at all an easy aria to pull off. Among the finest performances of it is that by the American-Greek singer Maria Callas who had a truly remarkable voice.

Pinkerton does return to Japan but Butterfly's optimism is disastrously misplaced and his visit leads to tragedy . . .

'Dolorosa' from *Stabat Mater*
1736
Giovanni Pergolesi (1710-1736)

Stabat mater dolorósa
juxta Crucem lacrimósa,
dum pendébat Fílius.

Here is a wail of motherly anguish. Mary is at the bottom of the cross where her son is being crucified. She stands there crying while he hangs above her.

There are 12 movements, beginning with the 'Dolorosa' sung by two singers, usually an alto and a soprano, although sometimes a choir is added. They take it in turn to sing the 13th-century text, going backwards and forwards, sometimes their notes temporarily clashing (a term known as 'dissonance') to reflect the tension in their terrible upset, before returning to sweet harmonies. It's haunting, but it's also very beautiful.

The piece was not written to be sung in public in church but as a commission by the aristocratic Cavalieri della Vergine dei' Dolori fraternity for use on Good Friday in the private chapel of San Luigi di Palazzo in Naples. Previously they had been using Italian composer Alessandro Scarlatti's arrangement but were looking for a more modern approach.

Despite some initial criticism when it was first performed in 1736, Pergolesi's *Stabat Mater* was probably the most printed piece of music in the 18th century. It is also probably the last piece that he wrote. He had made his name as the man who transformed opera from being a rather stately musical form into something more accessibly musical and singable with his short work *La Serva Padrona* ('The servant mistress'). He may even have finished it on his deathbed where he passed away at the awfully young age of 26.

The *Stabat Mater* has been set to music by many classical composers, including Antonio Vivaldi and Arvo Pärt. Pergolesi's 'Dolorosa' has also been arranged memorably as a mellow piece of jazz by the Victor Alcántara Trio, and as a relaxing dance track by Sasha Lazard who renamed her lilting version 'Stabat Mater IXXI' following the 9/11 attacks.

'Pie Jesu' from *Requiem*
1982
Andrew Lloyd Webber (1948–)

Given his background in musical entertainment with shows like *Cats* and *Jesus Christ Superstar*, it's no surprise that Andrew Lloyd Webber's *Requiem* is a little more theatrical than traditional versions, featuring a synthesiser, maracas and marimba. It's serious music but with his trademark captivating writing; it's not often that part of a requiem in Latin becomes a popular single and gets to number 3 in the charts.

He wrote it partly as a response to the death of his father, the equally talented composer William, in 1982, and also after reading in the media about genocide in Cambodia and atrocities committed during the Troubles in Northern Ireland. The text is a mix of the 'Pie Jesu' and 'Agnus Dei' parts of the standard Latin Mass, an appeal to Jesus, the Lamb of God, 'who takes away the sins of the world, Give them rest'.

However, the agnostic Lloyd Webber has shied away from calling it a specifically 'religious' piece, hoping instead that it is simply moving. He has described it as 'primarily a contemplation for myself',[7] for an audience of today, and certainly he did not anticipate its international fame. The back-and-forth between the female and boy soprano soloists is delightful – Lloyd Webber has suggested it's something like a brother–sister relationship.

The result was a smash hit as soon as it was premiered in 1985 with soloists Sarah Brightman and boy treble chorister Paul Miles-Kingston. Many artists, including Katherine Jenkins, have also recorded the work and it has become a common song to be played at funerals and memorial services.

'Pavane pour une Infante Défunte'
1902
Maurice Ravel (1875-1937)

The pavane is a slow dance that reached its height in the 16th century, a stately opportunity – often at the beginning of grand occasions – to show off the attendees' finery as they processed in a decorous manner around the ballroom.

Three hundred years later, Frenchman Maurice Ravel was finding his feet as a composer in Paris but when he premiered his 'Pavane for a Dead Princess' in 1902, it catapulted him to prominence. Indeed, like several other composers in this book, although he wrote many other works, he became so well known for this one piece that he developed something of a minor dislike for it.

Written initially for solo piano, it has become popular in the version he made for orchestra in 1910 with solos for the French horn, flute and harp. From the start it's gently melancholic with a strong dose of nostalgia. The dreamy melody is almost childlike in its simplicity and repetition, although it develops into something more spacious and lush.

Ravel was very particular about how the 'Pavane' should be played. The sense of restraint is written into the score with several notes to the player to 'hold back' written into the score. While it is intended to be played slowly and even at one point is marked 'super slow', Ravel was upset when pianists played it too sedately: he once said that it is a dead princess, not a dead pavane. Tommy Dorsey's swing orchestra certainly didn't play it very slowly in the 1939 arrangement renamed 'The Lamp is Low' with lyrics added by American songwriter Mitchell

Parish ('Dream beside me in the midnight glow, the lamp is low'). It continues to inspire 21st-century musicians – it's one of William Orbit's chilled-out *Pieces in a Modern Style* from 2000, and Hayley Westenra gave it another renaming and set of lyrics for her 2004 album *Pure* as 'Never Say Goodbye'.

Although it's very moving, strangely that wasn't really Ravel's intention. It's dedicated to the French Princesse Edmond de Polignac whose musical salons Ravel regularly attended, but Ravel said he only made up the title to sound poetic and that it wasn't intended to portray grief over a child's death. Instead, he imagined it simply as a recreation of the kind of dance a little princess in the 16th-century Spanish court might have danced. Even knowing this, it's still a very affecting piece.

'Music for a While'
1692
Henry Purcell (1659–1695)

> Music,
> Music for a while
> Shall all your cares beguile.

Sometimes you just want to listen to something sad. Sometimes you want something that recognises your sadness but provides comfort to ease it. Henry Purcell's 'Music for a While' does exactly the latter – a hint of melancholy but offering a solution too.

Purcell is in the running for the title of 'finest English composer ever'. A couple of years after his terribly early death at the peak of his career, the famous 17th-century diarists Samuel Pepys and John Evelyn listened to a recital of his music at Pepys' home in London and Evelyn noted in his diary that 'Mr Pursal' was 'esteemed the best composer of any Englishman hitherto'.[8] His fame has continued undiminished ever since.

'Music for a While' is a perfect example of Baroque music, featuring the harpsichord and a repeating bassline (known as a 'ground bass', one of Purcell's signature elements) for the bass viol, which is somewhere between a cello and a violin. The lyrics sung slowly over this are from a version of Sophocles' play *Oedipus* set to music by Purcell. At this point in the action in Act III, the terrifying Greek goddess Alecto with her eyes dripping blood and her Medusa-style snaky hair is calmed by the song; Alecto lets go of the whip she uses for punishing those who kill their parents, and the snakes drop away.

It's a clever piece of songwriting and literal word painting. In the line 'Till Alecto free the dead from their eternal bands', the word 'eternal' is really stretched out, while the 'drop' in the subsequent line 'Till the snakes drop from her head' is repeated nine times with the notes falling to represent the action on stage.

The finest recording is by Alfred Deller, the 20th-century counter-tenor with the delicately pure other-worldly tone, who did so much to popularise Elizabethan lute songs and Purcell's music in particular. It's mesmerisingly understated. The King's Singers offer a lighter version, which really accentuates the bassline and the 'drop'.

If this piece of Purcell isn't sorrowful enough for you, try his 'Dido's Lament' ('When I am laid in earth') from his opera *Dido and Aeneas* which has more ground bass and is a weapons-grade weepy.

'Adagio' from Cello Concerto in E minor
1919
Sir Edward Elgar (1857–1934)

The First World War caused an unimaginable level of death and injury and hurt. For English composer Sir Edward Elgar, it felt like the end of the world. On top of his disillusionment with life – he had written virtually nothing during the war at his home in his beloved Malvern Hills – in the following two years he underwent painful throat surgery, and his beloved wife Alice died. Yet at the same time he also wrote some of his finest work, including his much lauded Cello Concerto.

While it is a subdued elegy to a lost past, Elgar also makes it an electric listen. There is deep loneliness here as the cello and the orchestra explore the main theme together, but it is all done with tremendous spirit. Indeed, Elgar did not regard it at all as a complete misery fest and some recordings, such as the 1928 one with Beatrice Harrison as the soloist overseen by Elgar himself, are much brisker and less maudlin.

The work has a double dose of sombre overtones because of its association with the extraordinarily talented young cellist Jacqueline du Pré, portrayed controversially in the 1998 film *Hilary and Jackie* by Emily Watson. As she was establishing herself internationally, du Pré developed multiple sclerosis in her late 20s. She was forced to stop performing and died in 1987, aged just 42. Although the piece has been recorded by other cello titans including Steven Isserlis, Julian Lloyd Webber and Yo-Yo Ma, her interpretation played at times incredibly slowly and quietly is regarded as the most poignant.

The Cello Concerto had a disastrous premiere thanks to a

negligent conductor. It was Elgar's last major work as he meandered into semi-retirement and while generally respected, his reputation took something of a nosedive until the 1960s. As he neared the end of his life, Elgar whistled the main theme of the piece to a friend and told him that: 'If ever you're walking on the Malvern Hills and hear that, it's only me. Don't be frightened.'[9]

Main theme from
Schindler's List
1993
John Williams (1932-)

German-American composer and conductor André Previn often used to admonish jokingly his friend and fellow countryman John Williams that he should have the ambition to step away from writing film scores and return to operas and other classical compositions. To no effect. Classical music's loss has been film music's gain, and in his soundtrack to the 1993 movie *Schindler's List* Williams produced perhaps the best-loved examples of the genre ever written.

Williams and Steven Spielberg have worked together in nearly all the director's films including *Saving Private Ryan*, *Raiders of the Lost Ark* and *Jaws*. However, Williams initially found his first viewing of *Schindler's List* so moving that he doubted his abilities to score it. Spielberg insisted and it won Williams a host of awards – including his fifth Academy Award.

The intense main theme has become instantly recognisable around the world and the Israeli-American violin virtuoso Itzhak Perlman who plays it on the soundtrack says it is the one piece of music he is always asked to play, wherever he is performing on the planet.

The haunting, passionate violin theme appears throughout the film, which tells the true story of German businessman Oskar Schindler. He employed more than a thousand Polish Jews in his factories, saving them from removal to Nazi concentration camps. Williams was partly inspired by Jewish folk music and the main theme is particularly resonant because the violin was one of the instruments that prisoners were allowed to play in the camps' hastily assembled orchestras. Miraculously, some of these violins have survived.

Williams said he deliberately didn't want to go for anything too melodramatic, aiming instead for something that was more loving and gentle, more like a lullaby, a foil to the Nazi heartlessness. So while the sense of grief in the music is strong, it is also ultimately hopeful. The soundtrack is perhaps all the more emotional for the sparing use of it in the three-hour film, its reappearance right at the end, as Schindler's memory is commemorated by the survivors, timed to perfection. It colours the black-and-white movie rather than dominating it.

'Elegia'
1985
New Order

With a well-regarded first album under their belt the Salford group Joy Division were about to embark on their first US tour and seemed to be on the point of making the big time in 1980. But after struggling with health problems, depression and a problematic marriage, its charismatic lead singer Ian Curtis took his own life.

The group disbanded immediately but re-formed with a slightly different line-up as New Order. Five years later, on their album *Low-Life*, Peter Hook, Gillian Gilbert, Stephen Morris and Bernard Sumner released their musical tribute to Curtis, 'Elegia'.

It's a five-minute instrumental piece (though now also available in an 18-minute version with a climactic guitar section), a touching acknowledgement that Curtis's vocals were key to Joy Division's success, and one of their more fragile tracks. Although he was gone, his memory was still very much with them.

'Cantus in memory of Benjamin Britten'
1977
Arvo Pärt (1935-)

Benjamin Britten's death on 4 December 1976 shook Estonian composer Arvo Pärt badly. It was not just the scale of the musical loss to the world at Britten's relatively young age, but also because he had been looking forward to meeting the English composer, having only recently come across his work. This piece is his memorial to Britten.

It begins and ends with silence, a bookending that is actually written into the score. Then a funereal bell tolls and we're into a unique style of music developed by Pärt that he named 'tintinnabuli' (deriving from the Latin word for 'bell'), a format that mixes chant with minimalism to produce a contemplative sound resembling a bell. He called it his 'search for unity'.

There are some interesting effects in the piece, including variable playing speeds – in one section the violins play 16 times faster than the double bass – and all through it a bell continues to ring out. From a quiet start, the instruments feel like they are spiralling repeatedly and increasing in volume until, by the end, they are playing 'fortississimo' or 'very loudly'. Pärt often set religious texts to music and was interested in the idea of the relation between body and spirit. His intention with the 'Cantus' is to mark the voice parts (representing mortality) from the instruments (representing the eternal) and as the ultimate bell sounds at the end of the piece, the body's spirit moves on.

Pärt has talked about how music creates vibrations and how that resonates with us. One of the things he admired about Britten's music was its purity. This facet of his own writing shines through here. His melancholy is open to view, it's definitely an elegy, but also has a strong sense of commemoration.

'Cantus' was premiered in Tallinn and has since become one of Pärt's most popular compositions. It lasts just over six minutes yet feels timeless.

'Bathroom dance' from *Joker*
2019
Hildur Guðnadóttir (1982-)

Joker (2019) is an origin film that traces the downfall of wannabe standup comedian Arthur Fleck from failed performer to Batman's arch enemy. The music by composer Hildur Guðnadóttir won her an Academy Award making her the first Icelander to do so and the first woman to win solo for Best Original Score (Anne Dudley and Rachel Portman had won previously in the now defunct 'Best Original Musical or Comedy Score' categories). While she was writing it, Guðnadóttir was also working on the score for the *Chernobyl* television series.

Guðnadóttir collaborated closely with director Todd Phillips from the script to add her own musical thoughts to the film-making process rather than simply tacking the music on at the end once shooting was finished. In this way, she was better able to convey the melancholic breakdown of the character played by Joaquin Phoenix. As well as being a composer, Guðnadóttir is a distinguished cellist and that cello sound is front and centre throughout the film, coming to represent Fleck/ Joker. She also uses a 90-strong symphony orchestra, often virtually inaudibly, to add layers to the sound to match the layers that she saw in the lead character's psyche.

It's not a spoiler to say that the bathroom dance scene comes at a pivotal point for Fleck after a major turning point in his life. Closing himself away from the disintegrating city in a badly lit, run-down public toilet, instead of raging at the world he starts a slow and self-composed dance. And as he dances, we realise we are watching him as he begins a metamorphosis into his Joker personality.

It's a really simple but soul-wrenching piece led by the cello – actually a halldorophone, rather like an electric cello, which creates an element of feedback – with a light choral backing. As it progresses, the music becomes darker and darker as the Joker emerges. It's a hard but hypnotic watch, improvised by Phoenix on set, listening to Guðnadóttir's music using an earpiece on every take to inspire his neo-balletic performance. It was, in fact, the first piece that she wrote for the film, her initial gut reaction to the main protagonist, and Phoenix has admitted this scene was a turning point in his understanding of the character. According to Phillips: 'Arthur is one of those people that has music in him.'[10]

Main theme from *The English Patient*
1996
Gabriel Yared (1949-)

There are some lively tunes on the Academy Award-, Grammy-, Golden Globe- and BAFTA-winning soundtrack of *The English Patient* (1996). A bit of Fred Astaire dancing 'Cheek to Cheek', some Benny Goodman enjoying the 'Wang Wang Blues', while Lebanese composer Gabriel Yared's track 'Convento di Sant'anna' is a beautiful piece of illumination.

Yet the film is far bleaker, a tragic tale of love and betrayal in Italy and North Africa, set in the 1930s and 40s. From the very beginning of the credits, Yared presents us with a mournful solo played by Christine Pendrill on the cor anglais (an extended relative of the oboe), and a few notes from the harpsichord as a biplane rushes across the dunes of the Sahara Desert. We also hear for the first time the remarkable voice of Hungarian folk musician Márta Sebestyén beginning the haunting song about lost true love, 'Szerelem, Szerelem'. Unless you speak Hungarian, it's not at all clear what she's singing about but there is a definite sense of ambiguity about it – the film's director Anthony Minghella chose it because he liked the rootlessness of its sound. The song reappears in the film when Ralph Fiennes's character Almásy jokily explains it to Kristen Scott Thomas's Katharine who mistakes it for an Arabic folk song. While it talks about love, as he tells her, it also makes a connection with the sea that is important to the film, which he does not.

Minghella, himself an excellent musician, was keen for Yared, flushed with success from his work on the film *Betty Blue*, to give his score an Oriental/Middle Eastern ambiance. Yared was involved from the very beginning of production and early shooting sessions. The result was a mosaic of a soundtrack with numerous themes weaving in and out that matched the film's wandering structure. The 'Main Title Theme', which orchestras now play in concerts, is a wonderful blend that offers a touching five-minute précis. It's not overly dramatic but in its subtle wistfulness, it is powerfully desolate.

'Adagio for Strings'
1936
Samuel Barber (1910-1981)

Sandwiched between the pacy first and third movements of Samuel Barber's String Quartet is the 'Adagio', a marking which indicates it should be played slowly. It's not just slow, the nine-minute second movement is also universally recognised as one of the saddest pieces of music ever written.

Starting with sombre violins, the violas and then the cellos take their turns in this uneasy examination of grief. The music evolves subtly then reaches an intense climax and falls silent before reappearing. Barber's inspiration was a passage from Virgil's long poem the *Georgics*, written around 30 BC, which describes a mighty wave crashing onto rocks, churning up what was at the bottom of the sea into huge swirls. It's a decent description of how some people feel after listening to the 'Adagio'. Barber realised the heart-wrenching power of the piece immediately and wrote in a letter to a friend that he had just finished what he called 'a knockout'.[1] Thirty years later he set the music to words for choir using the section of the Latin Mass known as the 'Agnus Dei' ('Lamb of God, who takes away the sins of the world, have mercy upon us').

Composed in 1936, the wordless 'Adagio' quickly became synonymous with outpourings of grief at funerals (those of US Presidents Roosevelt and Kennedy, Albert Einstein, Grace Kelly), and most recently memorials for those who died in terrorist outrages (9/11, Charlie Hebdo, Manchester Arena bombings). The 'Adagio' has also been featured in many films, most poignantly in *Platoon* (1986), set during the

Vietnam War, which is at least in part the reason for it becoming linked to antiwar sentiments. It's America's unofficial music for mourning.

While it is very sad, and performances of it have become progressively slower in an attempt to really go for the heart strings, there is also an element of catharsis in the music. It's not hopelessly grim – Barber certainly never intended it to be so – and it feels as if a process of working through is involved in listening to it.

Perhaps the universal emotion it evokes is the reason why Barber's composition has found a new life as a dance track. William Orbit's chilled-out version on synthesiser is an interestingly dignified cover, and two Dutch DJs have also played around with it to great popular acclaim – Ferry Corsten's would not be out of place as background music in a gym, and Tiësto's pumped-up anthem is virtually unrecognisable.

INSPIRATIONAL

'Fugue' from
The Young Person's Guide to the Orchestra
1945
Benjamin Britten (1913-1976)

English composer Benjamin Britten often wrote his songs and operas for specific performers, in particular his partner, the tenor Peter Pears. He also wrote a number of pieces for children, including the short operas *The Little Sweep* (1949) and *Noye's Fludde* (1958), and *Friday Afternoons*, a 1935 collection of songs for the pupils at the school in Wales where his brother Robert was headmaster. In addition, he often included major roles for children within his mainstream operas and these gave actors David Hemmings and Michael Crawford their first tastes of the entertainment industry at a young age.

Writing good music for children is no easy task but Britten managed to achieve it without being at all condescending and the truth is that these works for a young audience can be enjoyed just as much by adults.

His major work for children began life as a commission for an education documentary about music but has found lasting fame as *The Young Person's Guide to the Orchestra*, first performed in 1946. It very much does what it says on the tin. Sometimes performed with short narrations to stitch it all together, it starts with the composer's arrangement for orchestra of Henry Purcell's catchy but splendid 'rondeau' dance from his 1695 music for a play called *Abdelazer*. This piece is then gradually dissected.

First of all we hear each of the main musical families play: woodwinds, brass, strings, and finally percussion. Then listeners get the chance to hear individual instruments play more than a dozen variations on that main theme, starting with flutes and piccolo, moving through bassoons and double basses, to trumpet and tuba, before numerous percussion instruments including the whip and the tam-tam gong get their opportunity. At the end, the instruments and families gradually reassemble in layers to play a lively racelike version of the original theme. It's educational in the broadest sense of the word – there's not a hint of a blackboard in sight here, just excellent music.

Britten's enthusiasm in encouraging children to learn about and love music has continued long after his death. He cofounded the annual Aldeburgh Festival in Suffolk in 1948, which not only puts on music performances but also runs various programmes for young musicians.

'Tonight' from *West Side Story*
1957
Music by Leonard Bernstein (1918-1990), lyrics by Stephen Sondheim (1930-)

It's hard to exaggerate the impact *West Side Story* had on the musical world when it opened in New York in 1957. Critics praised the exciting dances, the ambitious plot grappling with contemporary issues of racial and youth cultures, and the vivaciously catchy, sometimes almost operatic, music and lyrics.

One of the stand-out songs is 'Tonight'. It comes as the two rival gangs, the Puerto Rican Jets and the white Sharks (standing in for the Montagues and the Capulets from Shakespeare's *Romeo and Juliet* source), prepare for a 'rumble' later that evening. While the two gangs sing about their preparations, Maria and Tony, who belong to opposing sides in the conflict, only have thoughts for each other. All they're interested in is meeting up that evening as they explain in their touching duet ('Tonight, tonight, I'll see my love tonight.'). The couple sing about time moving so slowly for them just as the threats of violence seem to accelerate swiftly out of control. Sadly, the optimistic romance is about to hit the rails as Tony gets involved in the fight that follows.

The song is also cited as one of the examples of Bernstein and Sondheim's collaboration at its most operatic. The various characters and groups sing in turn, but then over each other in 'Tonight', quite oblivious of the others and announcing very different intentions - it's actually marked in the music as a quintet with chorus. It's reminiscent in particular of the 'Bella figlia dell'amore' ('Beautiful daughter of love') aria in Giuseppe Verdi's 1851 opera *Rigoletto* when a quartet sings about their four quite different aims.

It's irrelevant whether *West Side Story* is a musical or an opera (if there is any difference at all; they're both musical theatre). 'Tonight' is simply a remarkably powerful song of love and passion.

'The Ecstasy of Gold' from
The Good, the Bad and the Ugly
1966
Ennio Morricone (1928-2020)

Since 1983 heavy metal band Metallica have been introduced to the stage at their concerts by the same song. A fast rolling piano thrusts the music forward, as a solo oboe begins its call. In flutter the violins, a bell clangs. Singer Edda Dell'Orso's beautiful wordless half-wailing half-whooping rings out (known as 'coloratura' in opera) replacing that melodic oboe. The theme rises to a crescendo as a marching drum beat mimics a horse's galloping hoofs. Chiming bells clash, an electric guitar twangs . . .

'The Ecstasy of Gold' is one of Italian composer Ennio Morricone's most stirring tracks from all of the hundreds of films he scored. Metallica cofounder James Hetfield certainly agrees. When Morricone died, Hetfield posted on Instagram about how much the music pumped up the band and audience, that 'it has become a part of our blood flow, deep breathing, fist bumping, prayers and band huddle pre-show ritual'. The Ramones and Motörhead also used it for similar reasons.

It appears at an appropriately rousing moment in the 1966 spaghetti western *The Good, The Bad And The Ugly* (represented by Clint Eastwood, Lee Van Cleef, and Eli Wallach, respectively). After a long quest, Tuco, played by Eli Wallach, is running around a vast graveyard in the desert, desperately searching for a tombstone that he believes to mark an enormous stash of gold. The music is a perfect match for his wild desperation as he can almost hear the treasure calling out to him. It's the emotional high point of the film.

It's not surprising that the music and the action are so tightly connected since, very unusually for a film score, Morricone wrote the music before the movie was actually shot rather than adding it at the post-production stage. Director Sergio Leone loved the way that music told a story and used it to guide the emotions of the audience. He even played it to the actors as they were performing their scenes so that the action could be choreographed to the music. The duo repeated the process for the film *Once Upon a Time in the West* in 1968, which again featured the Italian singer Dell'Orso in sparkling form, and collaborated on five films in total.

Twenty years later, Morricone turned to the oboe once more to provide the popular plaintive theme to *The Mission* (1986), 'Gabriel's Oboe'.

'Maestoso' finale from the 'Organ Symphony' 1886
Camille Saint-Saëns (1835-1921)

Babe the pig is feeling distinctly under the weather. So Farmer Hoggett takes him onto his lap and feeds him some water. As it takes effect, he begins first to sing to him: 'If I had words to make a day for you, I'd sing you a morning golden and true' and then he dances. It's a tremendously moving moment in the 1995 film *Babe* and an equally rousing tune. It is, in fact, the finale to French composer Camille Saint-Saëns' Symphony No. 3, known as the 'Organ Symphony'.

In a highly competitive field of musical child prodigies, Saint-Saëns was perhaps the most precocious, arguably even more so than the more famous Mozart (see pages 53 and 133). Although he had wide interests, he dedicated his life to music and the 1886 'Organ Symphony' is his finest work, the 'Maestro' at the top of his game. It features nods to the great composers Georges Bizet and Johann Sebastian Bach (see page 254), and uses features of Gregorian chant in the finale. 'I gave everything to it I was able to give,' Saint-Saëns said. 'What I have here accomplished, I will never achieve again.'[12]

Despite its title, the organ is absent for about half of the half-hour long symphony. Saint-Saëns himself described it accurately as a 'symphony with organ', although in 2020 lockdown organist Jonathan Scott performed his own tremendous version of the whole symphony for solo organ.

The organ's biggest impact comes in the fiery finale, which has been described by Charles Nove, who loves to feature organ music on Scala's weekday breakfast show, as 'thunderously wonderful'. The theme has already appeared earlier, but here it's overpowering. A huge C major chord paves the way for the theme's return as part of a booming, exhilarating ride which really does raise the roof when performed in a cathedral or turned up high in the car to keep your mind focused and alert. Marked 'forte' or loud, organists usually give it much more oomph even than that.

Opening toccata to *Orfeo*
1609
Claudio Monteverdi (1567-1643)

This is where opera started. With some pretty loud trumpets.

In 1609 Italian composer Claudio Monteverdi published what he called his 'favola in musica' ('tale in music') *Orfeo*, recounting the ancient Greek legend of the lovers Orfeo and Euridice, the fatal snakebite which condemns her to the underworld, and Orfeo's attempts to get her back. There were no overtures in the early 16th century so the toccata – from the Latin word *toccare*, meaning 'to touch' and indicating a rapid-fire warm-up – starts off this early Baroque masterpiece.

The original score calls for five trumpets, although these days this is sometimes adjusted in performances to include a trombone. It's essentially a swirling fanfare, probably inspired by military calls or ceremonies. Indeed, the original trumpeters were probably in the military since the trumpet was not regarded as a music-making instrument, and there are no trumpets anywhere else in the opera. It's not entirely clear why an opera set largely in the countryside should start with such a dramatic flourish, although it's likely that it indicates Monteverdi's on-message willingness to help the contemporary revival of the ideals of medieval chivalry. It may also simply be that it is not really part of the opera, rather a heads-up to the audience to start paying attention or a welcome to attending nobility.

Monteverdi's lack of musical markings leaves plenty of room for interpretation for how these trumpets should be played. Using period instruments, they can sound pretty dramatic, though some conductors prefer to make it more majestic or lively.

While this is a big moment in the development of the trumpet, the original score includes some instruments that are much less well known today. The sackbut, an early version of the trombone, can still be heard at concerts of early music, but the double harp, cornetto (a kind of trumpet) and regal (a portable organ) are not in regular use.

Whatever the rousing toccata's purpose, *Orfeo* is the oldest opera still performed today, the first time that text (by Alessandro Striggio, 1537–1592) and music were meshed together to complement each other in this way.

'O Radiant Dawn' from *The Strathclyde Motets* 2007
James MacMillan (1959-)

Hastily assembled online choirs were among the most popular ways of getting together virtually during the coronavirus pandemic lockdowns in 2020. The Stay at Home Choir, created by musicians Tori Longdon and Jamie Wright, was among the most popular with more than 7,500 participants. Its recording, in collaboration with the choir The Sixteen, of 'O Radiant Dawn' by Scottish composer Sir James MacMillan attracted more than 700 amateur and professional singers from 72 countries.

MacMillan's strong Catholic faith often plays an important part in his compositions, such as *The Strathclyde Motets*, original settings of the Mass for religious occasions, from which 'O Radiant Dawn' comes. It is written to be performed towards the end of Advent, using an English translation of the traditional Latin text from 'O oriens'. 'O Radiant Dawn,' it appeals, 'Splendour of eternal Light, Sun of Justice, come, shine on those who dwell in darkness and the shadow of death.' The word 'come' is repeated in a growing crescendo to spectacular effect and the simplicity of the message shines through.

Like other modern settings of traditional church music, for example *O Magnum Mysterium* (see page 97), it packs an enormously emotional punch. MacMillan's music is a deliberate homage to the work of earlier composers such as Thomas Tallis and indeed the first four notes are a musical quotation from his 'O Nata Lux' (see page 34).

Though written for Advent, the message of 'O Radiant Dawn' – of waiting for a new beginning – has come to resonate very strongly for society at large and it is not surprising that it is MacMillan's most admired choral work.

'Maple Leaf Rag'
1899
Scott Joplin (c. 1868-1917)

Ragtime is one of the most infectious styles of music, guaranteed to have you smiling, humming and tapping your toes in seconds with its syncopated rhythms played off-beat. Its origins are a bit uncertain but it was particularly popular at the end of the 19th century and early decades of the 20th century when it became a nationwide craze in the US.

Its most famous practitioner was Scott Joplin whose 1899 'Maple Leaf Rag' was one of his first compositions but it has gone on to become arguably the most famous example of the genre. 'The Maple Leaf,' Joplin said, 'will make me the king of ragtime composers.'[13] He asked for it to be played at his funeral.

Like many rags, there are various repeating themes within its four sections, alongside some hearty piano-playing, as it leaps around. It's a tough one to do justice to, even for excellent pianists – there is a piano roll recording by Joplin at the end of his life which, despite illness forcing some mistakes, he takes at quite a speed. A few years after Joplin published the music, lyricist Sydney Brown added words telling a story about a poor man astonishing the rich people attending a dance in a ballroom. This is also tricky to perform since it's a very fast song.

Although some classical composers experimented with rag, such as Claude Debussy in his 1908 *Children's Corner* (see page 48), there was a long hiatus before ragtime became popular again in the 1970s. Pianist and musicologist Joshua Rifkin released a Grammy-nominated album of Joplin's rags, closely followed by the slightly anachronistic use of 'The Entertainer', also by Joplin, in the 1973 film *The Sting* starring

Paul Newman and Robert Redford set in the 1930s. Snooker fans will also recognise 'The Black and White Rag' written by George Botsford and performed by Winifred Atwell as the theme tune for the popular British television series *Pot Black*.

'Attaboy'
2011
Stuart Duncan (1964-), Yo-Yo Ma (1955-), Edgar Meyer (1960-) and Chris Thile (1981-)

Music critics sometimes excitedly throw terms around like 'genre-defying' when they're not really deserved, but in the case of *The Goat Rodeo Sessions* (2011), it's bang on.

A 'Goat Rodeo' is a polite term for a terribly chaotic, though not definitively unresolvable, situation. The premise for *The Goat Rodeo Sessions* does sound like it could be messy – a quartet of world-famous string virtuosos producing an album that offers an eclectic pick 'n mix selection of bluegrass, classical, blues, Celtic and jazz – but the result is quite the opposite: chamber music for the 21st century.

The four American musicians involved are classical cellist Yo-Yo Ma, bluegrass fiddler Stuart Duncan, double bass player Edgar Meyer and Chris Thile on mandolin. It's Thile's mandolin that leads off the album's first track, 'Attaboy', with Duncan providing a background drone on the violin. Ma – the only one of the quartet not known for his improvisations – provides the main melody. Inconspicuous musical cement comes from Meyer's plucked and bowed bass. Then it all hots up as Duncan, who calls the track a 'snowstorm of information', offers a violin jig and the music speeds up. The beauty is that while all the performers are remarkable solo performers, they gel really naturally. In fact, they all sat in a circle to rehearse and record the album to make the playing really intimate and connected.

'In the end,' Yo-Yo Ma says, 'what we're trying to do is simply make music that transcends whatever roots or categories or backgrounds that it starts from – that just exists as something that we're trying to express, through our community of values, as a moment in time creating very special music."[14]

It's certainly special music, winning a Grammy for best folk album, and reaching number one in the US Billboard charts in the bluegrass, classical and classical-crossover categories.

'The Liberty Bell March'
1893
John Philip Sousa (1854-1932)

American conductor and composer John Philip Sousa was a patriotic American who liked to reflect his devotion to his country in his music. So it's not immediately obvious that he would have given his wholehearted approval to his 1893 march 'The Liberty Bell' becoming the theme tune to *Monty Python's Flying Circus* (1969–74).

The slightly adapted *Python* version was chosen by its only American member, Terry Gilliam, partly because it was not in the slightest bit comedic (though of course that's all changed now). It's a rousing military march, the bell at the beginning putting the musicians through their paces and tubular bells throughout used to recreate its ring. Sousa had originally intended the piece to be included in one of his operettas, *The Devil's Deputy*. However, he changed his mind and with it the name of the piece, after visiting an exhibition in Chicago which featured a painting of one of the most important symbols of American independence and later the anti-slavery campaign, the Liberty Bell.

It was well received immediately and shows no sign of a drop-off in its popularity, becoming a mainstay of US Presidential inaugurations over the last two decades. Arrangements for banjo and mandolin/ guitar are particularly popular, although the Pythons chose the full orchestration as performed by the Band of the Grenadier Guards.

If it's unsure whether Sousa would have endorsed the Monty Python usage of 'The Liberty Bell March', it's even less likely he'd have been amused by what has happened to his 'The Stars and Stripes Forever' - although it's now the national march of the US, it has also become the tune to the football chant: 'Here we go, here we go, here we go.'

'I Was Glad'
1902
Sir Hubert Parry (1848-1918)

While there is room for some variation in the music at the coronations of British monarchs, since the days of Charles I they have always included 'Laetatus sum' or 'I was glad' in English. Using the text from Psalm 122, it prays for the peace and prosperity of Jerusalem and its use in the ceremony implies the same hopes for Britain. Leading composers over the centuries including Henry Purcell (see page 273) have had a crack at the whip and in 1902 it was Sir Hubert Parry's turn for Edward VII.

It's a stunning piece that really resonates, the organ (sometimes replaced with a trumpet fanfare and full orchestra) laying down sturdy foundations at the very beginning before the choir booms out majestically 'I was glad'. It's a very visceral moment and for that first coronation it was sung by a choir of 430 men and boys. The music becomes more lyrical in the second half of the work before returning to its full-blooded climax.

Parry used a pared-down version of the psalm – technically known as a 'choral introit' - and his setting has been used in all coronations since, though that first one in 1902 was nearly a disaster. The new king's entry was rather prematurely indicated to the choir, so they started too soon and finished before Edward VII had arrived. Being professionals, the organist Walter Alcock delivered something he improvised on the spot and the choir simply repeated part of it again until they were all back on track.

Parry spent more time as a music educator and administrator than as a composer. His most famous other work was also centred on Jerusalem. His setting of William Blake's poem 'And did those feet in ancient time' (1916) is widely sung on many occasions, although it was written to support the suffragette movement for which Parry campaigned rather than with any nationalistic overtones in mind.

'Heart-Shaped Box'
1993
Kurt Cobain (1967-1994),
covered by Hackney Colliery Band

Brass bands go back some 150 years in Britain and from the start had a strong connection with the workplace. Some, like the Black Dyke Mills Band, were sponsored by local companies but many more were associated with mining communities, such as the Grimethorpe Colliery Band which inspired the 1996 film *Brassed Off* for which they also provided most of the soundtrack.

There are not that many collieries in London's Hackney, but that hasn't stopped the intrepid nine-piece Hackney Colliery Band led by Steve Pretty to rejuvenate the concept of a 21st-century brass ensemble. With a jazz background and a hectic gigging schedule, they have brought their sound to a whole new receptive generation of listeners. Although much of their music is original, they do dabble in intriguing covers such as Blackstreet's 'No Diggity'. One of their finest is their take on Nirvana's 'Heart-Shaped Box'.

The original song written by the group's frontman Kurt Cobain appeared on their final album *In Utero* (1993), inspired by Cobain's romance with Courtney Love and his sadness at reading about child cancer sufferers. It was also the last song he performed live with Nirvana before his death in 1994.

The beauty of the Hackney Colliery Band's cover is that while it's quite a departure from the original and the trumpet replaces the vocals, it retains not only the same riff but also the essence of Cobain's song and its sense of vitality. And where Nirvana's version had the sense of menace that threads through many of their songs (it was initially called 'Heart-Shaped Coffin'), this cover is rather more upbeat. It's respectful to the original, but it definitely brings something new to the game.

'Fortune Plango Vulnera' from *Carmina Burana*
1936
Carl Orff (1895–1982)

Music doesn't get much more dramatic than this.

The unpredictability and fickleness of fate was a common theme in medieval writings. One of the most common ways of depicting it was as a random wheel of fortune – one moment you're king of the castle, the next you're bottom of the heap. These sentiments were central to a mostly anonymous collection of more than 250 poems dating back to the 11th century, mainly in Latin but also in German, called the *Carmina Burana*. Although transience is a key theme, the songs also focus on more worldly joys of drinking, eating, gambling and lovemaking. It's also the source for the tune to the Christmas carol 'Good King Wenceslas'.

In 1936 German composer Carl Orff reassembled these into his *Carmina Burana*, a 'cantata' (music for voices and orchestra) made up of 24 songs but with a similar combination of subjects. Although his music is entirely original, there is a strong medieval feel, often of foreboding, to it.

The cantata begins with warnings about the perils of providence. 'O Fortuna' is a magnificent start – slow, dark and substantial – with plenty of percussion (the triangle gets a really good workout) and a breathy chanting choir. The lyrics complain about the fickle power of Fate that waxes and wanes like the Moon, destroying everything in its path. As the rhythmic stirring music gathers pace in 'Fortune Plango Vulnera' the words describe how Fortune gives then treacherously takes away, that she seems to have a full head of hair but when you try to catch a ride on it, you're faced with an ungrippable bald patch.

You may be enjoying prosperity now, it continues dispiritingly, but the wheel turns and down you fall as somebody else is raised high. To cheer us up slightly, the next piece in the sequence is called 'The Merry Face of Spring' and is much livelier.

While it is the full-blooded singing and vigorous orchestration that has made the *Carmina Burana* famous, Orff also throws in some almost unreachably high notes for the baritone and soprano parts which are quieter though equally disquieting. But just performing the music itself wasn't dramatic enough for Orff who wanted it to be staged in a more spectacular way with some kind of action or dance on stage, an approach known as theatrum mundi or 'theatre of the world'. Most modern productions do not follow this style.

Orff's *Carmina Burana* is the first part of a trilogy called Trionfi ('Triumphs'), the second and third based on poems by ancient Roman and Greek writers Catullus, Sappho and Euripedes. These are also strikingly dramatic but far less hummable.

'Finding the Pattern'
from *Everybody's Gone To the Rapture*
2015
Jessica Curry (1973-)

Just as the emergence of movies offered composers a chance to flex their creative muscles in previously impossible ways, so the rise of the gaming industry has provided musicians with new possibilities. One of the most inventive of them is Jessica Curry.

Curry has worked on ground-breaking augmented reality projects with The Royal Shakespeare Company and she cofounded UK games developer The Chinese Room, which released the thoughtful *Everybody's Gone to the Rapture* in 2015. It sits somewhere between a novel and a game, the story following the mysterious disappearance in 1984 of everybody from the fictional rural Shropshire village of Yaughton. The player moves, quite sedately, around the superbly recreated village to discover just what is going on and why there are so many unexplained lights drifting around . . .

From the very beginning, the game was built in tandem with the music to aid the storytelling. This is not a score which has simply been tacked on to something that's already been done and dusted. With the lack of characters, Curry's BAFTA-winning soundtrack with glorious choral arrangements plays a very important part in creating an emotional soundscape for this very English apocalypse. This is a score that fans of Ralph Vaughan Williams (see pages 139 and 155) will love, with plenty of lush strings and nostalgic woodwind.

On 'Finding the Pattern', there is also the remarkable soprano Elin

Manahan Thomas who sang at the wedding of the Duke and Duchess of Sussex in 2018 and whose voice Curry has described as 'as close to the divine as I think I'll ever get'. Though Curry is not religious, the lyrics Thomas sings on this track come from Psalms 13 and 19 and offer hints about the game's resolution.

> How long wilt thou forget me, O Lord? For ever?
> How long wilt thou hide thy face from me? . . .
>
> Their line is gone out through all the earth,
> and their words to the end of the world.

Like the music throughout the game, it's slightly melancholic but there's no reason why everything inspirational has to be relentlessly upbeat. The soundtrack is a really fine match for the game, with certain themes interactively illuminating specific characters, objects or locations. Even so, it also works very well as a piece in its own right – and Scala Radio's resident video games music expert, Luci Holland, would agree. She loves playing Jessica Curry's inspirational scores in her weekly show 'The Console' because 'her work reaches deep into your soul when listening both in and outwith games, and is an example of the power games music has to elevate the story and experience through sound.'

Symphony No. 3 ('Eroica')
1804
Ludwig van Beethoven (1770-1827)

When he began writing the 'Eroica' in 1802, Beethoven was starting to go deaf. In fact, it had become so troublesome that he wrote his will and considered suicide, but didn't go through with it because he felt he had a musical destiny to fulfil. This time of struggle was a turning point for the German composer and he poured these mixed emotions into creating his new symphony.

It's an epic work, with a heroically confident first movement that starts with a bang, followed by its virtual mirror image, a slow second with an emotional funeral march. This has been used at many funerals and memorial services including composer Felix Mendelssohn's in 1847 (see pages 120 and 191) and US President John F Kennedy's in 1963. Then Beethoven introduces an energetic third movement (with fabulous hunting horn section requiring three French horns) and finishes with a joyous fourth that plays around with musical variations on a simple central theme. He was trying to write something that fitted what he optimistically believed was a brave new world of Enlightenment, something that in the shadow of the levelling aspects of the recent French Revolution celebrated all aspects of human life and endeavour.

It was not only bold in its conception – music as food for thought rather than just entertainment – it was revolutionary in its length, coming in at around 50 minutes, about twice as long as normal. It's monumental in every way.

Initially, Beethoven planned to dedicate it to Napoleon Bonaparte as he regarded him as the epitome of a new humanitarian and egalitarian approach to life. But when Napoleon proclaimed himself 'Emperor' Beethoven was disgusted, decided he was instead a tyrant (the composer was known for changing his mind about people abruptly) and literally scratched his name off the original score. He replaced its subtitle with the less specific 'Heroic Symphony, composed to celebrate the memory of a great man.'

'Cambridge, 1963' from
The Theory of Everything
2014
Jóhann Jóhannsson (1969-2018)

Icelandic composer Jóhann Jóhannsson wrote the score for the film *The Theory of Everything*, mixing traditional instruments with electronic elements to produce what he called soundscapes. He belonged to the modern minimalist movement, though his work is much more emotionally expressive than minimalist composers such as Philip Glass, as befits a musician whose heroes were Ennio Morricone and Bernard Herrmann (see page 185).

The biopic follows the English scientist Stephen Hawking's life from his time as an undergraduate, through the ups and downs of his diagnosis of motor neurone disease and marriage to Jane, through to being welcomed by the Queen to the Order of the Companions of Honour. As Hawking ages, the score deliberately does not reflect the changing popular musical trends through the decades, but maintains a timeless classical electronic sound, wholly appropriate in a film all about time. Also appropriate is the use of the piano that Jóhannsson selected for what he described as its 'mathematical-like quality'[15] and which is played by Scottish pianist Tom Poster.

From the very outset, we hear the four notes which will form what is essentially 'Stephen's theme', echoing again and again later in the film. It is, in fact, among the first pieces of music that Jóhannsson wrote for it. He called this the building block of the score and key in reflecting Hawking's zest for life. First it arrives as 'Cambridge, 1963', a beautiful loop of youthful power for piano and strings, where Hawking is a happy and robust student at university. It reappears immediately, rather slower, in the similarly sunny 'Rowing'.

Later though, it receives a less dynamic treatment. In 'The Stairs', it is much darker as Hawking is shown having difficulty climbing the staircase in his home. Here, Jóhannsson's musical experimentation is again apparent as he uses a Cristal Baschet, an organ made up of tuned glass rods which are played by rubbing with dampened fingertips.

Finally, as Hawking gives a lecture towards the film's end, the piece resurfaces in 'London, 1988'. It's a more serious variation, but reflective and wistful rather than schmaltzy melodrama. It's tasteful. And award-winning, scooping a Golden Globe as well as an Academy Award, a BAFTA, and Grammy nominations.

'Baba Yetu' from *Civilization IV*
2005
Christopher Tin (1976-)

Considering this was his first piece of music for video games, American composer Christopher Tin did quite well with 'Baba Yetu', written for *Civilization IV* (2005): it was the first video game music to be nominated for and win a Grammy. It was played at the signing of a peace accord in Mozambique. 'Baba Yetu' means 'our father' in Swahili (the national language of Mozambique).

Tin had already played earlier incarnations of the *Civilization* series, so was delighted to be asked to contribute music by his friend and games designer Soren Johnson. The song is written entirely in Swahili for choir and hand percussion (such as finger cymbals), the lyrics of the Lord's Prayer in translation starting: *'Baba yetu, yetu uliye Mbinguni yetu, yetu amina!'* Rhythmic, optimistic and immensely likeable, it has the anthem feel of *The Lion King* to it and has become a popular modern choral standard at concerts.

For the game 'Baba Yetu' was performed by Tin's former a cappella group, the Stanford Talisman, and by the Soweto Gospel Choir when he included it on his equally stirring concept album *Calling All Dawns*. Divided into sections tracing the cycle of life and rebirth, this is a truly international example of world music. Not only has it been used by the South African Premier League and the Vatican but the dozen songs are each in a different language, mostly taken from a famous work of literature produced in the country in question, and with more than 200 musicians from around the world involved in its production, including Portuguese fado singer Dulce Pontes.

Tin has also worked on film soundtracks – one is *Crazy Rich Asians* (2018) – and his 2020 album *To Shiver the Sky* looks at the history of flight from the ancient myth of Daedalus and Icarus to the moon landings. The opening track, 'The Dream of Flight', is a slight reworking from another major theme he wrote for *Civilization IV*, 'Sogno di Volare'.

Main theme from *The Adventures of Robin Hood*
1938
Erich Korngold (1897–1957)

If you need to explain to somebody what 'swashbuckling' means, it's probably simpler just to play them the two-minute opening theme to the 1938 film *The Adventures of Robin Hood* by Erich Korngold.

The film featured Errol Flynn in the title role at his charismatic peak (hooray!), wooing Olivia de Havilland's resourceful Lady Marian (hooray!) and duelling with the evil Basil Rathbone's Sir Guy of Gisbourne (boo!). Following them all the way was Korngold's glitteringly irrepressible soundtrack, sweeping the action along, very much foreground rather than background music.

Korngold was born in Austria and recognised as a child genius on a par with Mozart. With the rise of the Nazis, he went into self-exile in America just at the moment when talking pictures were beginning to take the importance of music in movies seriously. The first scoring Academy Award was awarded in 1934, and Korngold won it in 1936 for *Anthony Adverse* and then again for *The Adventures of Robin Hood*.

Korngold composed much of the score in his head and on the piano in his cabin while he travelled on an ocean liner between Europe and the US, but nearly called the whole thing off when he saw the first cut of the film. He said he wasn't good enough a 'musical illustrator' to do justice to what he felt was a '90% action picture' and only continued on the basis that he could give up at any moment if he felt it wasn't working.

It certainly did work. Korngold described his film scores as 'operas without singing' ('Opern ohne singen') and the 75 minutes spent around Sherwood Forest is riveting. Collaborating with a team of orchestrators under the direction of fellow composer Hugo Friedhofer, Korngold wrote and recorded the whole thing with a 65-piece orchestra in seven weeks, a considerable feat. To speed up the process, he recycled bits and pieces from his back catalogue – if you listen to his *Sursum Corda* symphonic overture written when he was just 21, you can hear very clearly where the opening trumpets in the main theme come from.

He was the first composer to bring the idea of a leitmotif – a recurring theme associated with individual characters – from the classical world to film composition. The bright and bold opening title theme previews some of these: the Merry Men's march, Richard the Lionheart's regal theme and the trumpet fanfare that signifies the Normans and the immoral Prince John (boo!).

Korngold encountered a considerable amount of snobbishness because of his work in Hollywood and, despite its obvious brilliance, his film music was rather discounted by the music establishment. The first recording of any of *The Adventures of Robin Hood* film music only appeared four years after his death and it's only in the last 30 years that his genius has been properly appreciated. Among film composer fans is modern maestro John Williams (see pages 93, 196 and 277).

NOTES ON SOURCES

Chapter One: Through a Day
Time Out & Sleep
1. Author commentary in CD booklet, www.hyperion-records.co.uk/ dw.asp?dc=W21684_GBLLH1960301
2. Multiple interviews including www.20jazzfunkgreats.co.uk/ wordpress/2015/12/invitation-to-dream-an-interview-with-max-richter
3. *New York Herald*, May 21, 1893 at web.archive.org/ web/20060923062509/homepage.mac.com/rswinter/ DirectTestimony/Pages/62.html
4. Jane Campion's *The Piano* by Jane Campion and Claudia Gorbman
5. Interview with Polygon, www.youtube.com/watch?v=iUaPHTC2
6. Composer's own website, www.jaakkomantyjarvi.fi/CVEN.html

Chapter Two: Events
Marriages
1. Ruth Barton and Simon Trezise, *Music and Sound in Silent Film* (Abingdon, Routledge, 2018) via planetradio.co.uk/scala-radio/ entertainment/music/pride-prejudice-carl-davis
2. danceartjournal.com/2019/11/30/thoughts-on-coppelia-the-royal-ballet
Deaths
3. www.hyperion-records.co.uk/notes/30017-B.pdf
4. Multiple obituaries, such as eu.usatoday.com/story/ lifemusic/2013/11/12 john-tavener-composer-and-seeker-dies-at-69/3508339
5. www.howardgoodall.co.uk/works/choral-music/eternal-light/a-21st-century-requiem
Major dates
6. CD booklet
7. Interview in www.theguardian.com/uk/2011/apr/29/royal-wedding-music-paul-mealor
8. www.chandos.net/chanimages/Booklets/AV2372.pdf
9. Richard Streatfield, *Revival: Handel* (Abingdon, Routledge, 2019)
10. Composer's own website, www.alexisffrenchmusic.com
11. Prokofiev wrote it originally in an article in 1934 for the Russian newspaper *Izvestia*, then it was included in S Shlifstein and Rose

Prokofieva, *Sergei Prokofiev: Autobiography, Articles, Reminiscences* (Honolulu: University Press of the Pacific, 2000) and is also quoted in *The Cambridge History of Twentieth-Century Music* (Cambridge, Cambridge University Press, 2004)

12. www.vulture.com/2017/12/the-story-behind-the-music-of-the-muppet-christmas-carol.html

13. An article by Lauridsen: www.wsj.com/articles/SB123516723329736303 and on his own website: www.mortenlauridsen.net/articles.html

Chapter Three: Activities
Books & Reading
1. Arthur Conan Doyle, 'The Red-Headed League' (Strand Magazine, 1891)
2. www.pepysdiary.com/diary/1662/09/29/
3. www.anthonyburgess.org/a-clockwork-orange/the-music-of-a-clockwork-orange
4. musiquefantastique.com/new-soundtracks/his-dark-orchestrations

Food & Drink
5. planetradio.co.uk/scala-radio/entertainment/music/scala-radio-sessions-live-composer-rachel-portman
6. Interview at www.heraldscotland.com/arts_ents/14215702.ale-carr-takes-rebellion-to-new-territories

Exploring Nature
7. The Household Division, www.householddivision.org.uk/perry-mason-notes
8. Eric Saylor, *English Pastoral Music: From Arcadia to Utopia, 1900–1955*, (Urbana-Champaign, University of Illinois Press, 2017)
9. Finch from her own website, www.catrinfinchandseckoukeita.com/bio
10. Keita in interview at www.theguardian.com/music/2018/apr/29/catrin-finch-seckou-keita-soar-review-senegal-wales

Transport & Travel
11. Originally appeared in *Essex Life & Countryside*, October 2001, mentioned at www.crime4u.com/existing/morendsixpseven.html
12. artandmusic.yale.edu/romantic-landscapes/mendelssohn-scotland/mendelssohn-gallery2-letter-his-family
13. In a letter, quoted in Roger Fiske, *Scotland in Music: A European Enthusiasm* (Cambridge, Cambridge University Press, 1983)
14. Press release www.soniafriedman.com/news-press/the-music-of-harry-potter-and-the-cursed-child-is-available-to-pre-order
15. The first quote, in *America Music* magazine, both included in Howard

Pollack, *George Gershwin: His Life and Work* (Oakland, University of California Press, 2006)

Chapter Four: Exercise
Walking
1. German National Tourist Board, www.facebook.com/germanytourism/photos/a.296891493819182/1247357772105878/?type=3

Running
2. *Apocalypse Now* (1979)
3. VSQ Biography, web.archive.org/web/20100220020025/http://vitaminstringquartet.com/about.html
4. From a KUOW radio interview web.archive.org/web/20120907234906/http://www.kuow.org/mp3high/mp3/KUOWPresents/20110115MartinODonnell.mp3
5. Mission statement at www.kaleidoscopeorchestra.co.uk
6. From an interview www.ign.com/articles/2016/03/23/how-the-beatles-influenced-the-halo-theme-song

Dancing
7. *Dance Magazine* (August 1931) and, more recently, in George Balanchine and Francis Mason, *101 Stories of the Great Ballets* (Anchor Books, New York, 1989)

Chapter Five: Moods
Peaceful
1. The programme notes are mentioned in Richard Greene, *Holst: The Planets* (Cambridge, Cambridge University Press, 1995)
2. Composer's own website philipglass.com/compositions/glassworks
3. Interview on CD, *Bernstein Century – Bach: St. Matthew Passion*, 1999 Columbia recording
4. Letter, quoted in Robert Orledge, *Gabriel Fauré* (London, Eulenburg Books, 1979)
5. twitter.com/OlafurArnalds/status/1093898498691485698
6. Mentioned in Gene D. Phillips, *Beyond the Epic: The Life and Films of David Lean* (Lexington, University Press of Kentucky, 2006)

Sad
7. Interview in *The Christian Century*, March 18–25, 1987
8. Evelyn's diary, mentioned in Margaret Willes, *The Curious World of Samuel Pepys and John Evelyn* (New Haven, CT, Yale University Press, 2017)

9. Director's video 'Anatomy of a scene' for *The New York Times,* www.youtube.com/watch?v=nTVdN6s3rXY

10. www.julianlloydwebber.com/2019/08/elgars-cello-concerto-centenary-year/ and Christopher Grogan, *Edward Elgar: Music, Life and Landscapes* (Barnsley, Pen & Sword History, 2020)

11. Luke Howard, 'The Popular Reception of Samuel Barber's Adagio for Strings', *American Music,* Vol. 25, No. 1 (Spring, 2007)

Inspirational

12. David Dubal, *The Essential Canon of Classical Music* (New York, North Point Press, 2004

13. Ray Argyle, *Scott Joplin and the Age of Ragtime* (Jefferson, NC, McFarland & Co., 2009)

14. Press release, www.sony.com/content/sony/en/en_us/SCA/company-news/press-releases/sony-music-entertainment/2011/sony-masterworks-celebrates-another-groundbreaking-sales-week-with-the-goat-rodeo-sessions.html

15. Interview at deadline.com/2018/02/the-theory-of-everything-composer-johan-johannsson-adds-a-timeless-touch-1201269263

UK/US GLOSSARY

autumn / fall
cinema / movie theater
curtains / drapes
football / soccer
garden / yard
holiday / vacation
jelly / jello

primary school / elementary school
pub / bar
railway / railroad
shop / store
sweets / candy
taxi / cab
university / college

Musical terms:

bar / measure
cor anglais / English horn
interval / intermission
orchestra leader / concertmaster or concertmistress

Major dates:

Guy Fawkes Day: an annual celebration in the UK that marks the arrest of Guy Fawkes, a member of the Gunpowder Plot, and the foiling of the attempt to blow up the Houses of Parliament in London on 5 November 1605.

Remembrance Sunday: taking place on the second Sunday every November in the UK, this is a day to commemorate British and Commonwealth military and civilian servicemen and women in the World Wars and subsequent conflicts.

INDEX

Abels, Michael 84–5

'Absalon Fili Mi' (des Prez) 132

'Adagio' (from Cello Concerto in E minor) (Elgar) 275–6

'Adagio for Strings' (Barber) 286–87

Adams, John 179–80, 227

Adams, Richard 239

Adler, Larry 16, 169, 195

The Adventures of Robin Hood (Korngold) 318–9

'Agnus Dei' (from *Eternal Light: A Requiem*) (Goodall) 67–8

Alcock, Walter 304

Allegri, Gregorio 80–1

'Allegro non troppo' (*Four English Dances*) (Arnold) 16

Allen, Woody 121, 140

'An American in Paris' (Gershwin) 197

'Andante quasi lento' (from *A Carol Symphony*) (Hely-Hutchinson) 98

Anderson, Marian 245

Aphex Twin 253, 265

Aristophanes 139

Arnalds, Ólafur 259

Arnold, Sir Malcolm 16, 195

'Arrival of the Birds' (from *The Crimson Wing: The Mystery of the Flamingos*) (Swinscoe) 173–4

Art of Noise 211

Ashington Colliery Brass Band 40

Ashton, Frederick 115

Asplund, Tommi 224

'At the Castle Gate' (Sibelius) 205

'Attaboy' (Duncan/Ma/Meyer/Thile) 301–2

Attenborough, David 175

Atwell, Winifred 300

Austen, Jane 55, 76

Avatar, main theme from (Horner) 171–2

'Ave Maria' (Mäntyjärvi) 43

Avicii, DJ 228

'Avril 14th' (Aphex Twin) 265

'Baba Yetu' (Tin) 316–17

Bach, Johann Sebastian 165, 227, 254–5, 294

Balfe, Lorne 127–8

Ballets Russes 112

'The Banks of Green Willow' (Butterworth) 158–9, 162

Barber, Samuel 219, 286–7

Bardac, Emma 47, 48

Bardac, Régina-Hélène (Dolly) 47, 48

Baring-Gould, Sabine 211–12

Barnum, P T 48

Bart, Lionel 145–6

Batchelar, Martin 160

'Bathroom dance' (from *Joker*) (Guðnadóttir) 282–3

Batt, Mike 239

Bax, Clifford 249

The Beatles 132, 218

Beaumarchais, Pierre 54

Beck, Karl 232

Beecham, Sir Thomas 205, 237

Beethoven, Ludwig van 76, 144

Symphony No. 3 ('Eroica') 312–13

ACKNOWLEDGEMENTS

We hope you've enjoyed *A Soundtrack for Life* and that you've discovered more about your favourite classical pieces and discovered new favourites too! This is Scala Radio's first book and we're really proud of it – just as we're proud of everyone in the team, so we're going to take a moment to sing their praises here!

First, many thanks to the team at Kyle Books for approaching Bauer's National Radio Brands Marketing Director Clare Baker shortly after the station launch in May 2019 with a brilliant idea for a book. Special thanks also to Alex Johnson for being such a welcoming collaborator with Scala's Head of Music Jo Wilson and Programme Manager Jenny Nelson.

Thanks to our presenters who share their love of classical music with our listeners every week: (in alphabetical order) Angellica Bell, Hannah Cox, Jamie Crick, Alexis Ffrench, Anne Frankenstein, Luci Holland, Sam Hughes, Mark Forrest, Mark Kermode, Simon Mayo, Charles Nove, Jack Pepper, Darren Redick and Penny Smith.

More thanks to the consistently hard-working, positive and creative members of the 'behind the scenes' team at Scala Radio (in alphabetical order): Sebastian Clark, George Cooper, Poppy Davenport, Lissie Day, Izzie Gardner, Jon Jacob, Mark Jeeves, Cat Martin, David May, Alice Millar, Phoebe McFarlane, Amelia O'Shea, Steve Taylor, Tom Watters and Laura Jane Wilson.

Special mentions to Steve Parkinson, Ric Blaxill, Anne-Marie Lavan, Leanne Wallis, Susan Voss, Chris Vezey, Tony Moorey, the team at Think Farm and Dee Ford for their guidance, advice and vision!

And most importantly, thanks to the Scala Radio listeners who have discovered us on digital radio across the UK and embraced a new classical music and entertainment radio station. Whether you've been a member of the Scala Radio family since the start, or you've only just found us, this book is dedicated to you!